We tend to succumb to dissatisfaction and discouragement unless we are able to live as pilgrims at heart, longing for our home in eternity.

Elizabeth-Anne Vanek

PILGRIMS AT HEART

Scriptural Reflections, Prayers and Poems

Elizabeth-Anne Vanek

Living Faith Publications • St. Louis, Missouri

"Brookend," "Cracked Chalice," "Infinity," "Lazarus," "Plenitude," "Quest," and "Who Is The Christmas Christ?" are taken from *Frost and Fire*, Copyright © 1985 by Elizabeth-Anne Vanek. Used with permission.

"Apophatic," "Ashes," "Desert Places," "Dry Wood," "Grasping Grace," "Ordinary Time," "Quickening," and "Wounds" are taken from *Extraordinary Time*, Copyright © 1988 by Elizabeth-Anne Vanek. Used with permission.

"Creation," "Nailed," and "Perpetuum Mobile," are taken from *Woman Dreamer*, Copyright © 1989 by Elizabeth-Anne Vanek. Used with permission.

International Standard Book Number: 0-9629585-3-0
Cover design: Chris Strahan
Cover photo: Bob Pool
Interior illustrations: Annie Scheumbauer

Printed in the United States of America

*For the people of
St. James Parish, Chicago,
who so graciously welcomed
my family when we were in need of
a place to worship,
and who continue to offer us
a spiritual home.*

Contents

Introduction

Many readers of this book may remember a time when reading the Bible was considered "Protestant." Catholics in those days prayed by "going to Mass"; the extent of our familiarity with Scripture was listening to the Sunday Gospel reading or meditating on the life of Jesus through the rosary, Stations of the Cross or other devotions. Since the Second Vatican Council, however, Catholics have discovered that there are many ways of praying and that Scripture, in particular, offers a powerful way of encountering God.

There are as many approaches to God's word as there are people who pray. For some, the events of Jesus' life hold the most meaning; for others, it is encountering him in his roles as teacher, healer and friend; for still others, it is exploring the rich symbols so intricately woven through both Hebrew and Christian Scriptures. Some people like to "get under the skin" of a biblical character and reconstruct, in their imagination, a favorite scene. Some prefer to take a short passage and read it over and over again until the words sink into the heart. Others bring their own lives to the experience—suffering with Jesus in the Garden of Gethsemane, for example, or praying with the psalmist for deliverance from the pit, or rejoicing with Mary in the singing of the Magnificat.

My response to God's word is heart-centered. As a poet with an active religious imagination, I find myself intuitively understanding what I read, being profoundly moved by it and then somehow responding to it in oral or written form in such a way that others, too, say they find their own religious imaginations activated. God's word becomes my word, felt in the deepest part of self; this is the word that I present in this collection of my Scripture reflections, prayers and poetry.

An editing project originally led me to immerse myself in Scripture. Because my two children seldom slept, even as infants, I became accustomed to doing most of my free-lance work late into the night. One project involved the basic grammatical editing of a horror novel, but one cannot "fix sentences" without absorbing content. I would find myself physically ready for bed at about 2 a.m., but I could not sleep because of the unnerving images I had encountered during my work (I have never been able to stomach horror movies or violence of any kind). To clear my mind, then, I began reading Scripture and, in turn, writing poetry on Scriptural themes, Scriptural reflections for my parish bulletin and, eventually, to writing for *Living Faith*. A quarterly booklet of daily Catholic devotions, *Living Faith* is the source of the Scriptural reflections and many of the prayers in this book.

I am the product of two cultures, each of which

has uniquely formed my religious imagination. Born into the pre-Vatican II Roman Catholic Church of the 1950s, raised both in England and on the Mediterranean island of Malta, I am aware of northern as well as southern European influences in my life. On the one hand, I experienced anti-Catholic sentiment in England and my classmates looked down upon me because my mother is Maltese; on the other, in Malta I observed rather than participated in the rich island legacy of saints, fireworks and baroque pageantry (my father is English, making me a perennial foreigner there).

Sundays in England meant being bored on a regular basis. I remember cold churches in which every woman wore a hat and an expressionless face. The Latin made no sense, the bells mystified, and I was left with a feeling of "having done the proper thing" without enjoying it. I was vaguely aware, even at an early age, that being Roman Catholic in England in the '50s was somehow counter-cultural, somehow anti-queen and country. I'm not sure where I picked up this notion, but I felt like a defender of the faith, and I refused to join in the unfamiliar prayers at my Protestant day school, dreaming of glorious martyrdom and concealing priests in secret passages, to save them from the gallows . . .

In Malta, every church, even in the poorest of villages, seemed like a magnificent cathedral. I would stare down the long nave to the distant altar, fascinated by the reflection of light on the silver candela-

bra and crystal chandeliers. The tapestries, oil paint-
ings and statues depicted various martyrdoms in
lurid detail; the marble pillars were draped in scarlet
hangings with gold fringes; the floor was a mosaic of
Latin-inscribed tombs, bearing family crests and limited genealogies. During Mass in the long, hot sum-
mers, I would squirm on my straw-covered chair,
often being attacked by vicious bugs as I waited,
impatiently, for the half hour sermon to come to an
end. Since I understood neither Latin nor Maltese, I
distracted myself as best I could with the Scripture
readings included in my missal.

Religion permeated the Maltese culture: statues
of saints were on every street corner, candle-lit shrines
on every country road, stone carvings on cemetery
walls of souls burning in Purgatory, gaudy pictures
of Jesus and Mary inside every bus. Little wonder
that I felt drawn towards mystery; little wonder that
I began to see the Holy Land in terms of the Maltese
landscape with its olive and carob trees, its prickly
pears and oleanders, white rock and Mediterranean
blue . . .

The boarding school I attended on the island
was also spiritually formative. Run by the Sacred
Heart sisters, the convent offered a fine arts curricu-
lum on which I thrived. I wrote plays and performed
in them, participated in debates, gave speeches to
visiting dignitaries, went on archaeological digs, and
studied classical literature. Most importantly, the
school offered sacred space in which I could simply

"be" and explore my relationship with the indwelling God. Whether participating in community prayer in the chapel or spending time alone under the palm trees in the quadrangle or on the convent's farm land, I felt nurtured and alive. When the liturgical changes of Vatican II were introduced and immediately incorporated into school liturgies, I felt privileged to participate in the new ways and was energized by the sweep of the Spirit.

As important as the spiritual life was to me, I never saw myself involved in any kind of Church ministry or even knew this was an option. By the time I graduated from high school, I had only encountered one or two women who held professional positions or who had even attended university. I embarked on a degree in English because this seemed the most practical option. I had no dreams for the future, or any expectations that I would ever find a niche in the professional arena, let alone Church work. The women I knew were, for the most part, content to live vicariously through their husbands. Status and wealth were the main goals to which anyone aspired.

The surprise of my life came when I fell in love with a Peace Corps volunteer—my husband, Jim—and found myself getting married the day after my twenty-second birthday and moving to Chicago. Taken out of the narrow future I had envisioned for myself, I was plunged into endless possibilities. At first, my response to my new environment was limited: I experienced culture shock, homesickness and wondered, at times, whether I would ever survive being 7,000 miles away from my family. Depression set in; my only release was prayer.

Shortly after arriving in the States, I began a Masters degree in English, became pregnant with Peter, our eldest child, and looked to a future that would be academic in nature. I began teaching English part-time, assuming that Peter, when he arrived, would simply sleep or play on demand while I began a doctoral program. This did not happen. By the time I was 25, I had two degrees, one baby and another (Alexia) on the way. I was exhausted. Inevitably, parenting plunged me into a new way of being. I delighted in family life, particularly in creative play with the children. I learned flexibility and patience, but also became aware of a vague restlessness within myself. The question began to surface: what was I going to do with my life?

Gradually, I began to weave different activities into my domestic world: teaching, writing books of poetry, volunteering on the parish liturgy team, giving presentations at other parishes and schools, completing an internship in spiritual direction and gaining a Doctor of Ministry degree from the Graduate Theological Foundation. While my life may read like a frenetic list of activities, much work has been going on beneath the surface—painful work, at times, involving grappling with spiritual issues and coming to terms with past experiences. Though outwardly appearing to be over-extended or compulsively busy, I have learned to take the quiet time I need for my own nurturing—and when to say "no."

At times, I am surprised at how much I am actually doing, until I remember that it is God who is "doing the doing" through me. I am conscious of being used to empower others, conscious of doing much for which I never received training, conscious of the effortlessness for most of what I do. Sometimes, I am amused by God's sense of humor—using me, a very unlikely candidate, to reach out to the many who happen to come my way. For this, I have a deep sense of gratitude, but it also prompts me to remember that my primary commitment must be to my relationship with God: for unless God is at the center of my life, nothing else makes any sense whatever.

The liturgy of my life—my own sacred story—and the liturgical calendar are intricately woven together in the reflections, prayers and poems offered in this collection. I would like to think, however, that my presence in these pages is simply that of a "background" against which readers can see the tapestries of their own lives; I hope that my insights will lead others to insights of their own, that my theological reflection is not an end in itself, but a beginning point . . .

There is no "right way" to approach this book.

Delving into Advent during the summer months is quite appropriate, if one is in a place of waiting; praying through Lenten themes in the Christmas season could be useful if one is experiencing "the desert." On the other hand, following the liturgical divisions does provide the opportunity to enter each particular season more fully, if that is helpful. *Pilgrims At Heart*, like any other prayer book, is only a tool for the journey: eventually, all pilgrims must find their own way to the waiting heart of God.

ADVENT

. . . the starkness of the trees reminds me to enter into the nakedness of my own spirit, humbly and patiently.

The colors and fragrances of Advent have always drawn me to this season. Sarum blue, pinks and purples, candlelight and chants of longing have helped me keep watch, even as cultural signs have encouraged me to get busy. Paradoxically, this time of inner stillness—the stillness that is before birth—is also a time of frenetic activity. Barely before Thanksgiving is over, the merry whirl of Christmas parties swings into motion, and one is into shopping and baking, card writing and gift wrapping. Red and green predominate, baubles glitter in every window and the heavy fragrance of evergreen potpourri lures us into thinking Christmas is already here. But it is not...

I thank God for the waiting. I try to tune out the voices which clamor, "spend, spend, spend, rush, rush, rush..." and to focus instead on that still small voice within which says, "wait in simplicity." And here is the tension: while I desire this simplicity, the outer world drowns my senses in such lavish festivity that I begin to wonder whether Advent is ever possible. Each time I drive down a neighborhood street, venture into a shopping mall, or turn on the television, I am reminded that the world does not run according to a liturgical calendar.

In chronological time, waiting is seen as an inconvenient trial, not a period of quiet growth in which each pause is a promise of something yet to come; worse still, inactivity is regarded as "non-productivity"—few stop to think that one can be "acted upon" (by God, of course) in the inactivity or that there is value in passivity. To suggest that waiting is a spiritual exercise or that the fullness of Christmas comes only to those who are unafraid of emptiness seems like folly to a world which thrives on immediate gratification.

At times, discouragement sets in, but then, before I become entirely cynical, the gentle whiteness of a first snowfall helps me to become centered again; delicate traceries of frost upon the window panes invite me inwards; the starkness of the trees reminds me to enter into the nakedness of my own spirit, humbly and patiently. Even as I outwardly prepare for Christmas festivities, I move into silence and solitude.

To find monastic stillness on a university campus and within the noise of my own family is a challenge. In the workplace, there are the never-ending needs of students and colleagues; at home, there are electric guitars, rock music and rebellious teenagers. At times, the contemplative in me feels overwhelmed, completely frustrated, but then I remind myself that the desires of the heart are stronger than the obstacles to achieving them; and my heart's desire is to wait upon my God . . .

For me, then, it is the disposition of the heart which makes it possible to enter the stillness of

Advent. My own spiritual hungers create a sense of poignancy; my own struggle to carve out "prayer time" heightens my need for the reign of God in the here and now; my consciousness of the darkness of the world, both literal and figurative, awakens in me a longing for the presence of Light. As I reflect upon the incompleteness of the world, of my life, I am moved to acknowledge my utter dependency upon the God who broke into history by becoming one of us. I find myself drawn into the mystery of God's tender love, remembering yet again that with God all things are possible and that God can break into the smallest moment, despite hectic schedules and too much noise . . .

There is a purity to Advent that I find missing at other times of the year. It is not a season for either asceticism or jubilation; it is not a time for focusing on sin or redemption. Rather, it is a season of the heart's movement toward God, of God's movement toward the human heart. And all our waiting is for one end: to increase our capacity to be pregnant with the presence of the Christ Child.

Come, Lord Jesus!

A New Focus

Comfort, give comfort to my people.
                                    Isaiah 40:1

Too often we view Advent as a penitential season rather than as a time to re-focus our lives. We find ourselves caught between the culture's emphasis on externals and our own rigorous attempts to look inwards. The effort to observe a "mini-Lent" while Christmas shopping and listening to carols is often jarring.

Perhaps we would do better to abandon the struggle. Perhaps we need to stop trying to overhaul our lives and instead to focus on our relationship with God. Perhaps we need to "do" less in order for God to "do" more. There is just a chance that if we allow God to break into our hearts we may experience belonging instead of alienation, forgiveness instead of guilt, comfort instead of failure.

Speak tenderly to us, Lord, that we may hear your voice.

Great Longing

He has sent me to heal the brokenhearted.

Isaiah 61:1

Advent is not the season for those who are satisfied or complacent. It belongs to all who hunger for glad tidings. It holds promise for all who know themselves to be flawed. It calls us to rejoice and to hope precisely because we yearn for an alternative to life as we know it.

Advent is the season of great longing. It is the time for admitting incompleteness, inadequacy and fragmentation. It is the time for acknowledging our own woundedness and that of the world. It is never easy to confront pain. Often, we feel vulnerable because praying from the center of our pain can cause emotional havoc; we can become overwhelmed by the grief which surfaces when we speak to God about our needs. It is easier to sing out in praise than to cry out for healing, but cry out we must if the God of the brokenhearted is to enter our lives.

Shelter us, Lord, in your own wounded heart that we may find comfort.

Advent Prayer

There was a time—O God, do you remember it?—when I wanted answers straight away. There was a time when I looked for signs and tried to make bargains with you, thinking I could influence you in my favor. Now I know that all time belongs to you and that your ways are not my ways. Now I know that what you want is my love, not sacrifices. I believe in you, God; I trust you know what is best for me. Willingly, I put myself in your hands.

Opportunity For Grace

As to the exact day or hour, no one knows it.
Mark 13:32

The hour of fear or the hour of liberation? The hour of death or the hour of new beginnings? The hour of disgrace or the hour of splendor? Scripture readings about the "end times" or the coming of the Lord seldom leave us unmoved: the imagery of cosmic chaos is terrifying and yet there are also images of glory, brightness and resurrection. Whatever associations the Second Coming holds for us are sharpened by our ignorance of the time it will occur.

Each day brings both us and the world closer to ending; each day is also the opportunity for grace, an opportunity for preparing ourselves for whatever is to come. If we stand with the Lord, if we rejoice in holiness, wisdom and justice, if we long for the reign of God with an intensity which almost consumes us, the "end times" can represent promise, not dissolution. Seen in this way, death itself can be a source of limitless possibilities, not the curse of extinction.

Lord, help us to read the signs of your presence that we may be ready for your coming.

Reign Of Truth

Anyone committed to the truth hears my voice.
John 18:37

For most of us it is not easy to arrive at truth. We try to unravel the reality about ourselves, but there is always one more perspective that needs to be taken into account, or one more mitigating circumstance that we may have overlooked. Rigorous as we might be, we have to admit to bias and some blindness.

Jesus describes his reign as a reign of truth. As we progress in the Christian journey, we learn how to see things from God's perspective instead of our own. We learn to discard our habitual viewpoints and to risk a more radical view, one which may threaten all our preconceptions, prejudices and rigid attitudes. Freed from our own distortions, we begin to speak and act out of the conviction of right vision; we feel compelled to utter the words ringing in our hearts, even though this may disturb the status quo. And, surprisingly, whatever the consequences of speaking this word, we find ourselves set free by its liberating power.

Help us to see as you see, Lord, and to hear your voice in all things.

Spiritual Progress

Conduct yourselves in a way pleasing to God.
1 Thessalonians 4:1

Behaving "rightly" is often conditioned by ulterior motives. As children, we were exposed to a system of rewards and punishments from a very early age. We learned that while crying and shrieking occasionally brought results, smiling sweetly and saying "please" or "thank you" could be even more effective. Many were taught that both God and Santa Claus were omnipresent; piety became a guarantee of heaven and of a stuffed Christmas stocking. And if we are like most adults, we now "play the game" in the workplace, performing well to keep or enhance our jobs.

Progress in the spiritual life takes us beyond notions of rewards and punishments. If we pray because we expect a raise or a promotion, then we are praying to satisfy our own wants. If we treat others kindly because we hope God is keeping a score sheet, then we are not truly loving God or our neighbor. Only when we can forget about the self and behave "rightly" because this is pleasing to God, only when we learn to love without motives, will we be serving God fully.

Loving God, teach us to love you for your sake, without expectation of gain.

Presence Of God

The Lord is near. *Philippians 4:5*

I am perplexed by your nearness, Lord. At times, you are nearer than my very self: your presence envelopes me, possesses me, empowers me; whatever I do, wherever I go, there is no escaping your spirit. Your nearness claims me and I cannot resist. Everything else becomes unimportant, even irrelevant. My heart beats for you alone.

But there are other times, Lord, when you seem more distant than the stars. I try to pray and you are not there. I call out your name, but you do not respond. I struggle to imagine you beside me, but see only emptiness . . .

I have come to realize, Lord, that I have no control over your presence. You are always with me—that I know—but you do not always allow me to experience your nearness. However much I pray, however much I yearn to be one with you, I am sometimes still left feeling "orphaned." Help me to be humble, Lord, and to recognize your presence as a gift. Help me to be faithful, especially in those times when you seem most distant.

Remove from me, Lord, anything which blocks you from my sight, and let me accept you on your terms, not mine.

Constant Readiness

The foolish ones, in taking their torches, brought no oil along, but the sensible ones took flasks of oil as well as their torches.

Matthew 25:3-4

One does not need a scout's training to know the importance of being prepared. Few would take a long car trip without checking the gas or the map. Few would go camping in the wilderness without provisions. Few would brave the rapids without a paddle or life vest. It is only common sense to be equipped properly.

In the parable of the ten bridesmaids, only five are prepared. The oil they carry symbolizes the richness of their inner life; they are ready to meet the groom because there has always been a place for him in their hearts. They have lived in a state of constant readiness, so his arrival does not take them by surprise. Torches blazing, they sing and dance at the gateway, inviting him in. But the five foolish bridesmaids have cared only for passing delights. Discovering, too late, that the groom does not recognize them, they offer us an image of what it means to be foolish in God's eyes.

Teach us your wisdom, Lord, that we may be ready for your coming.

Plenitude

We prepare
and all our preparation
leads us to the knowledge
that we are not prepared.

We wait
and at the end of all our waiting
we find that nothing has changed;
we are the same.

We strive,
we struggle,
we gorge on the riches of Advent—
its colors
its music
its fragrance
until, satiated,
we know poorness.

We, the poor,
wait for the plenitude of Christmas
and are rudely let down
rudely deceived
because Christmas
is not all that we believed it was,
dreamed it was,
were told it was.

We, the poor,
balk at Christmas
because we choke on Incarnation.
We cannot comprehend . . .

Respond

Make ready the way of the Lord; clear him a straight path. *Mark 1:3*

Advent is the season of the pilgrim God, the God who hungers for our love, the God who intrudes into human history by being born as one of us. We often speak of our journey towards God, but, in reality, it is God who does most of the travelling. The God who is already present in the very depths of who we are draws nearer and invites us to respond. This God insists on breaking through the wasteland into the wilderness of our hearts.

This Advent, let us make God's path smooth. Let us remove all stones and boulders, fill in potholes and treacherous pits. Let us tear down all obstacles that stand in the way, especially the overhanging branches and piles of debris from crumbling walls. And then, when this is done, let us wait, quietly and peacefully, for the One who is to come.

Come, Lord Jesus; our hearts are waiting for you in readiness.

Lord Of The Least

Truly I tell you, just as you did it to one of the least of these who are members of my family, you did it to me. *Matthew 25:40*

Lord, I have seen you in the homeless ones, huddled in blankets outside revolving brass doors on New York's Fifth Avenue. I have seen you sleeping in cardboard boxes outside the White House, tourists averting their eyes as they go by. I have seen you stretched out in churches in downtown Chicago, swaddled in rags, surrounded by shopping bags. I have heard you croon to the street lamps, shaking your beggar's cup for a nickel, perhaps a quarter or two.

Yours are the desperate eyes of young criminals with no future, the tear-filled eyes of their victims, the pain-filled eyes of the sick and dying; yours the tears which fall over the graves of your friends.

Lord, there is not a day when I do not see you. I am overwhelmed at times. I try to reach out but there are so many needs, so much suffering. Remember my distress, Lord, remember how helpless I feel, and forgive me for what I have left undone, both now and at the hour of judgment.

Only you can wipe away the tears of the world, Lord. Let this be my comfort.

God's View

Would that all the people of the Lord were prophets! *Numbers 11:29*

We sometimes confuse prophets with fortune tellers—those whose particular psychic abilities enable them to reveal what is presently hidden from most of us. Sometimes, we limit our image of the prophetic voice to the rantings and ravings of hermits who emerge from their solitude only to attack the rest of society.

But prophecy is more than a prediction, more than curses howled into the night. The prophet's role is to point the way, to reveal reality, to encourage others to live with integrity. The prophet presents God's view of things to a world which would otherwise not take notice. The prophet's task is to "wake people up" to what is going on around and within them so that hearts may melt in compassion and wrongs be redressed.

Whether we recognize them or not, there are prophets all around us, prodding us with their words, teaching us by their example, revealing God's heart to the suffering world.

Let your word sound in our hearts, Lord, that we may be your voice to those we meet along the way.

A Child's Wisdom

The calf and the young lion shall browse together, with a little child to guide them.

Isaiah 11:6

Perhaps it is only a child's imagination that can bring together wolves and lambs, leopards and kids, lions and calves. Perhaps it is only in child's play that cows and bears can live in a peaceable kingdom or that babies can charm poisonous snakes with their innocence. In an adult world, there is little room for such fantasy: we would feel distinctly threatened without walls and cages to keep out the wild beasts, whatever or whoever they may be. We tend to desire security and comfort more than harmony. We prefer established boundaries to ambiguity. Being in control is at times more valued than anything else.

Making straight God's path, however, involves learning the wisdom of a child, so that we can break down all that separates us from each other and from our deepest selves. Reforming our lives involves learning to surrender to God's dream for humankind, that moment when we indeed become like little children, and there will be neither harm nor ruin on God's holy mountain. And a little Child shall lead us.

God of all harmony, may the wild and the tame browse together in your peace.

Steady Our Hearts

Make your hearts firm, because the coming of the Lord is at hand. *James 5:8*

Promise and patience go hand-in-hand in Advent's readings. Isaiah joyfully proclaims the saving presence of God, describing how even the land will burst into flower and song. James, on the other hand, advocates a posture of waiting; for him, God's work will be done in God's time. All *we* can do is wait.

But waiting gracefully is no easy task. Whether we are waiting for a new job opportunity or for the arrival of a baby, for a new home or for important news, it is hard to live in the present moment. Instead, we immerse ourselves in the future, counting the days and hours, worrying and wondering, hoping that all will turn out the way we dream it will. We know all too well the taste of dust and emptiness, the cruel letdown that comes when what we have waited for fails to materialize.

Jesus is the one who can steady our hearts. Jesus is the one who has come and who will come again. In him, all time is present tense; in him, our hope has already taken flesh. He is the Alpha and the Omega, the one beyond time and the one beyond waiting. He assures us that all will be well.

Let us find you now, Lord; let us remember that now is the time of salvation, not tomorrow.

Be Healed!

Then will the eyes of the blind be opened, the ears of the deaf be cleared. *Isaiah 35:5*

I have hearing, Lord, but I am deaf. I have sight, but I am blind. You came to heal all those with disabilities and I am one of them. Yes, I have the gift of physical wholeness, but I do not always see and hear and understand. I ask you now to unseal my ears and to open my eyes. I ask you to let me grow in awareness that I may see what is below the surface, that I may hear what is barely audible, that I may perceive what is almost imperceptible. Give me the gift of being awake, Lord. Jolt me out of apathy and indifference. Startle me out of my comfortable routine. Rouse me from all that buries me under blankets of habit.

Yes, Lord, I know there will be a price to pay. Yes, I know that reality can burn and that it is more comfortable not to see and not to hear. But I also know that sharper seeing and keener hearing will lead me to your life. Heal me, Lord. Comfort my frightened heart.

God of all healing, may the wholeness I seek be to your glory and delight.

Apophatic

Old Zeck was alone when it happened:
chosen by lot,
he hunched over the brazier,
muttering before the Holy Place
in his thin, age-cracked voice,
when the angel popped into view
and rudely interrupted.
Outside, the congregation prayed,
hoping their words would rise
like the sweet-smelling incense
burning within.
Zeck trembled, distraught
at the disturbance,
but the angel persisted in absurdity,
promising a son, an infant prophet,
to bring joy to the geriatric pair.
Skeptical but restrained, Zechariah
followed sacred tradition
by demanding a sign,
and mighty Gabriel,
burning bright at the right side
of the altar,
silenced him.

Hope In Uncertainty

Then people will see the Son of Man coming in the clouds with great power and glory.
Mark 13:26

While the "end time" may hold its own particular terrors, we don't have to wait for cosmic confusion to be gripped by panic. Though the stars may be fixed in place, though the sun may radiate light, dreadful happenings still shake the foundation of life for peoples everywhere.

Refugees, boat people, famine victims and the afflicted peoples of warring nations are only a few of those whose worlds have been shaken by catastrophe. Closer to home, we see lives shattered by poverty, disease, violence, accident and natural disaster.

The fact is that terror can strike anyone, anywhere, without warning; life, at its best, is tentative. Our hope in all this uncertainty is the presence of the risen Lord—that Lord who is more powerful than harrowing trials, that Lord who calls each of us to life in abundance.

O God, help me to trust you even when my heart may be trembling with fear.

Living With Ambiguity

Jesus answered, "My kingdom does not belong to this world." *John 18:36*

Kingdom paradoxes are puzzling. The kingdom is here, but it has yet to come in its fullness. The kingdom is now, but it is also a reality for which we must wait. The kingdom is somehow present in this world, but it is radically different from any of the political structures around us.

As subjects of this enigmatic kingdom, we need to learn to live with ambiguity. The might of our kingdom is built on service to the least of its members. The security of this kingdom rests not on weapons or battlements but on our vulnerability. The longevity of this kingdom is founded on truth and integrity. Yes, ours is a kingdom of the heart in a world that is obsessed with power, prestige and wealth. And our king—Jesus, the Crucified, the Alpha and the Omega—invites us into the quiet reign of his love. Paradox of paradoxes, in this kingdom, our greatest achievement will be to recognize that we are all God's children, and to treat each other accordingly.

May your kingdom come, Lord, in our own time.

New Growth

In those days, in that time, I will raise up for David a just shoot. *Jeremiah 33:15*

On these cold days when the northern hemisphere moves into the starkness of winter and the brilliance of autumn fades with the leaves underfoot, our Scriptures present us with an image of new growth. This shoot, springing up from the line of David, holds promise and invitation. It reminds us of the Child who burst forth from the Virgin's womb. It encourages us to find seeds of new life in the barrenness of our own hearts.

This shoot holds all the greening power of spring. Its roots reach deep into frozen soil. Its trunk thickens, its branches break into leaf, gently spreading over us. And we, safe beneath this canopy of green, feel a stirring within, the quickening of life, the desire for a Birth.

O God, may my heart always be a fertile ground for the seeds of new life you hold out for me.

A Shining Light

You are the light of the world. *Matthew 5:14*

Depression could be considered one of the major epidemics of the 20th Century. Brought on by fear and hopelessness, intensified by disappointment and loss, it can entangle all of us, young and old, without warning. The outer darkness which we see imaged in senseless violence, economic chaos and the exploited environment often becomes internalized. We grow weak and lethargic, susceptible to physical ailments, unresponsive to others' needs. The world is no longer home to us, but a hostile prison.

When we are caught up in outer darkness and weighed down by inner darkness, we can often see no way out. Time and time again, however, small rays of light surprise us into joy. Chance meetings, unexpected phone calls and small acts of kindness can rouse us from inertia, re-awakening in us the memory of what it is to be alive. Grateful for this deliverance, we need to let our light shine so that we, too, can help others again find meaning.

Come, Lord! Let your light rise for us in the darkness. Come, Lord! Let us be your light for others.

Full Of Joy

When Elizabeth heard Mary's greeting, the baby stirred in her womb. *Luke 1:41*

What stirs us? What touches us to the core, filling us with joy and hope? What so moves us that we become entirely radiant? What is the message that can awaken us, enkindle us and enflame us?

The Word of God when seen, when heard, when embraced and welcomed, makes our hearts leap within. That Word which we await is born in us each time we open ourselves to its mystery. It forms us and sends us forth; it schools us and nurtures us; it challenges us and comforts us; it invites us into joyful expectancy; it helps us to be full of courage; it sustains us through all the seasons of our lives.

May this Word take flesh in us that we may be ready for a new Birth. May Christ's coming find us pregnant with anticipation.

Come, Lord Jesus, make your home in our hearts.

Quickening

Ancient hungers kindle
untrammeled
by routine, things material
or franticness of days
crammed full
with motion.

The nascent god
stirs within,
life quickening
in space uncluttered,
burgeoning
in stillness
like a hidden seed
which swells,
then sprouts, bursts forth
in sudden splendor.

And with the stirring,
all hungers deepen . . .

Hear And Believe

Blessed is she who trusted that the Lord's words to her would be fulfilled. *Luke 1:45*

Christmas approaches. The time of birth is near. The season of waiting is almost over. In the final days of Advent, we can prepare ourselves by asking what words the Lord has spoken to us. Have we heard the scriptural proclamation of peace and joy and made it our own? Do we believe that this birth of 2,000 years ago holds promise for those of this era, for ourselves specifically? And if we have heard and if we have believed, what difference does it make to us?

Mary heard, trusted and found blessing. God spoke the impossible and she accepted, becoming in that instant the dwelling place of the Most High. In her, the Word was fulfilled; through her, the Word became flesh. We, too, need to listen in the stillness of our hearts to the words God whispers in our waking and in our dreaming. We, too, need to listen to that voice close as our own thoughts, constant as the rhythm of our blood. When will we hear?

God of all possibilities, make us pregnant with your word, with your presence, that your will may be done.

CHRISTMAS

The longer we can linger in the stable, the deeper our experience of Christ's coming will be.

As I ponder the meaning of Christmas, the word "pause" comes to mind. To "pause" is to open oneself to mystery and to reflect on ultimate meaning. I am not sure that our culture lets us "pause" to celebrate Christmas. The pre-Christmas rush carries us along at an unrelenting pace until it is unmistakably post-Christmas: the last baubles have been packed up, the poinsettias have withered, and browning Christmas trees are scattered in alleys. The feast has come, but did we stop to notice? The light has shone in the darkness, but have neon lights and glitter eclipsed it? The word has been spoken, but have radio jingles and TV specials spoken more loudly still?

I sometimes think that we avoid pausing. Were we to be fully present to God's revelation in this holy season, what would we find? A challenge to make different choices? An invitation to greater intimacy with God? More than we bargained for? For many of us, it may feel safer to indulge in merry-making and good cheer than to kneel in awe at the manger; it may be easier to tame Christmas into a birthday party for children than to look at the implications of the birth of the Holy Child in our own lives.

If we were to pause for a few moments, chances are that we would be totally overwhelmed. If we could gaze upon the Christ Child, and see in him the sacrament of God's love, we might find ourselves silenced in the face of this mystery: for God to take on human flesh and to enter the violence of human history as a defenseless baby is more than the mind can imagine; for God to suffer as each one of us suffers—to experience poverty, rejection and hatred—is beyond comprehension. In our gazing, we may just catch a glimpse of the length and breadth, the height and depth of God's love—and we may be moved to tears.

The shepherds and magi were people who paused that first Christmas. Their night's watch having been interrupted by angels, the shepherds abandoned sheep and fields and found their way to the humble stable. The magi, too, their star-gazing interrupted by a brighter star than all the rest, went in search of the newborn king. Upon finding their hearts' desire, both shepherds and magi knelt before the Holy Child. In spite of the squalor, the stench and the inevitable animal sounds, they recognized the presence of God in this most unlikely of places. Seeing, they believed; and believing, they gave worship. They paused long enough to allow the mystery of God's love to penetrate their hearts; and this was the gift which they carried away with them, the gift that made all other gifts seem empty of meaning.

If we allow the Christ Child to interrupt our agendas, what will *we* have to leave behind? If we find ourselves called to Bethlehem, what will we discover once we reach that holy place? And if we pause at the manger, what will we see contained within it? Seeking the "meaning" of Christmas involves asking ourselves these questions. Like the shepherds and the magi, we, too, need to let go of all that gets in the way of responding to the Birth—our busyness, for example, our anxiety, our partying, our cynicism, our pride, our anger, our addictions.

The call to journey towards Bethlehem is nothing less than a call to re-evaluate what is important to us and whether we are prepared to empty ourselves of everything that gets in the way of this call. Freed from our attachments, we can gaze upon the Child with greater clarity, seeing not just a fragile baby but God incarnate. Filled with wonder, we can cradle our God to our hearts, knowing that we, too, are held within that embrace.

The longer we can linger in the stable, the deeper our experience of Christ's coming will be. By pausing, we are asserting that God's time is more important than the passing of chronological time; by pausing, we learn to enter into the timelessness of God's presence where we discover that we have been loved from all eternity . . .

Come, let us worship!

Who is the Christmas Christ?

Who *is* the Christmas Christ?
A child!
A man!
A god!

One we leave in the cradle
because He is safer there

because He is easier to worship
there

because He is
less demanding there

and a child
fills us with the hope
that tomorrow might be easier
that tomorrow is worth waiting for
when we cannot bear
our todays.

We can dream on

without rebuke
plotting His destiny
—and ours—
like protective parents
who want to control
everything
so as to avoid
risk, pain, uncertainty.

And so,
in our wisdom,
we worship the Babe,
taming Christmas
into a birthday party for children
though we have not learned
to be children ourselves.
Who is the Christmas Christ?
A child.
A man.
A god.

The child
breaks free of His swaddling clothes,
and of *our* expectations,
surprising us
by being Himself.

The gentle snow
becomes a whirlwind storm

that disturbs
dismays
upturns households
shatters the status quo,
and beneath the tinsel and glitter
is more than we bargained for:
a child
a man
a god
THE REFLECTION OF WHO WE ARE

Out Of Darkness

The people who walked in darkness have seen a great light. *Isaiah 9:1*

The theme of light in darkness continues: it appears in the excerpt from Isaiah, a reading we hear during the Christmas Midnight Liturgy, and in the reference to it in a later Gospel passage (Mt. 4:12-33). Christmas and Ordinary Time, the child Jesus and the adult Christ, Spirit and Mission are somehow linked.

There is also another dimension. The Gospel account of Jesus' transition from private to public life includes the call of the first disciples. Simon, Andrew, James and John abandoned their fishing nets and followed Jesus without hesitation. It was as though they immediately recognized Jesus as the promised Light which would dispel all darkness. Jesus, for his part, recognized in them qualities which would enable them to share in his ministry.

Matthew tells us that Jesus taught in the synagogues, healed the infirm and proclaimed the good news. In time, the disciples would learn to do likewise. We, like them, have been called out of darkness to bring light to others. We also have been called to let go of what "ties us down" for the sake of the reign of God.

May the light of Christ shine in our hearts, wherever we may go.

Goodness Itself

The Lord, your God, is in your midst . . .
Zephaniah 3:15

There are days when there doesn't seem much to rejoice about. Sometimes specific events trigger sadness or apathy; at other times, these feelings surface for no apparent reason. We are conscious of being "out of joint," but we don't know how to let the mending begin.

Perhaps being "down" happens when we focus too exclusively on ourselves, our difficulties and limitations. When we grow in attentiveness to God's presence, then Divine Love becomes a cure for our self-pity. When we remember that God has power over all things, then we may find our own powerlessness more acceptable. And when we acknowledge that God is goodness itself, then we may feel less frustrated when our plans fall through and our lives take a different course from what we had dreamed for ourselves.

If we want to experience true joy, then we need to be present to the God who, continually rejoicing over us, invites us to the festival of love.

Help us to recognize your presence, Lord, even in the midst of darkness.

Broken-hearted God

As a bridegroom rejoices in his bride, so shall your God rejoice in you. *Isaiah 62:5*

The opening chapters of the book of Jeremiah present a broken-hearted God, trying to come to terms with the fickleness of the chosen people. ". . . like a woman betraying her lover, the House of Israel has betrayed me," says the Lord (Jer. 3:20).

We seldom think of God as one who can be moved by our actions, but these lines portray a passionate, intimate God, not an indifferent observer. God weeps over fallen humanity, rejoices in redeemed humanity, and is, in turn, desolate and ecstatic.

Incarnation is the ultimate proof of God's excessive love. Creator becomes creature, dwells among us, shows us the pattern of holiness so that we, too, can make the heavens rejoice. Incarnation is God's pledge to be involved.

Let the Lord delight in us, now and always. Let Christmas find us with hearts of flesh, not stone.

Glimpses Of Light

**But who will endure the day of his coming?
And who can stand when he appears?**
Malachi 3:2

For Anna and Simeon, the awaited day happened when they were well-advanced in age. This day was the answer to the hopes and prayers of generations. This day gave meaning to years of expectations. In the form of a child, this day presented God's own redemptive word. Having cradled the child in their arms, both Anna and Simeon were content to die.

Few people are privileged to encounter ultimate meaning so powerfully. For most of us, God's breakthrough into our lives happens in small, sometimes imperceptible ways. We have glimpses of light scattered here and there. We have moments of understanding which punctuate our habitual dullness. We receive insights through half-forgotten dreams. We experience heightened awareness in the middle of frenetic schedules.

If our lives are open to mystery, if we learn to pay attention to the hints and guesses of God's presence among us, then we, like Anna and Simeon, can find contentment.

Dear God, keep me always open to the many and mysterious ways of your coming into my life.

Epiphany Moments

The Lord, the Lord, a merciful and gracious God, slow to anger and rich in kindness and fidelity.

Exodus 34:6

A literal reading of the Bible leaves us with the impression that patriarchs, prophets and other leaders had greater access to the reality of God than we do today. Which of us, after all, have heard God's voice burst from the clouds or from the heart of a burning bush? Which of us have seen signs and wonders that defy natural laws or rules of logic?

The temptation is that we can get so caught up in the drama of biblical portrayals of revelation that we miss epiphany moments in our own lives. God reveals who God is in ways which are subtle and easily missed. God speaks in the whispers we hear in the depths of our own hearts or in the dreams we barely remember upon waking. God directs us with hints and guesses, with gentle prods rather than with Hollywood-style flamboyance. If we are attentive, however, we will see and hear, taste and touch that mystery of gracious love which holds us all in its embrace.

Open our eyes to your presence, Lord, that we may find you in all the days of our lives.

God's Light Is Constant

I will make you a light to the nations, that my salvation may reach the ends of the earth.

Isaiah 49:6

The plane shudders and lurches through dark clouds; the floor beneath my feet vibrates. As we move deeper into turbulence, I feel both queasy and afraid. Anxiously, I look out, over the wing, for patches of brightness. I need the security of the sun.

Whenever there is darkness, we tend to grope towards light, or, at the least, to hope for it. Dreary winter days are tedious and depressing and make us long for springtime. Inner darkness likewise weighs heavily and makes us yearn for peace. "Won't this storm ever pass?" we ask. "Will spring never come?" So accustomed are we to darkness that we begin to doubt whether light even exists.

As I stare out of the plane window, I try to remind myself that God's light is constant, no matter how dense the storm clouds. I try to remember that the only real darkness is that darkness in which we fail to recognize the saving presence of Jesus, Light of Light, true God from true God.

Let us see your light, God, even on the darkest days.

Walk In The Light

Let us cast off deeds of darkness and put on the armor of light. *Romans 13:12*

Deeds of darkness suggest secrecy, shame and fear, the chains of sin, the power of evil; they are what we reject every time we remember our baptismal promises; they represent all we must let go if we are to progress in our journey—not only destructive patterns of behavior, but crippling attitudes and unhealthy attachments.

St. Paul urges us not simply to "let go" but also to "put on." The darkness of the shroud must be replaced by the mantle of Christ's light. It is not enough to purge ourselves of darkness and to be people of the twilight; rather, we need to be bearers of light, revealers of light, so transparent with goodness that we are images of God's beauty to those around us. "Come, let us walk in the light of the Lord!" cries Isaiah. Come! Let us be light! Let us shine in this season of the birth of God's light!

Clothe us in your light, God, that we may bear your light to others.

The Light Of Christ

Magi from the east arrived in Jerusalem, saying, "Where is the newborn king of the Jews?"
Matthew 2:1-2

The seekers are the finders in the Gospel for the Epiphany. Because they are serious about their own inner journeying, because they can distinguish between signs and what they signify, the astrologers make progress in their quest. Ultimately, they find both the star and the Christ Child. Having asked probing questions of themselves and of the cosmos, they are ready to receive the answer to their deepest longings.

Herod, on the other hand, is incapable of co-existing with either the star or the one to whom it points. He would rather destroy the child than change himself or the old order.

As we celebrate the feast of the Epiphany, we need to ask ourselves whether we most resemble the magi or the frightened king: are we committed to star-quests or do we hold mystery at bay?

O God, you show your light to those who truly seek you; give me a curious yet open and trusting heart so that I may see your light when it shines forth in the world around me.

Perpetuum Mobile

And so the wisemen
have completed their journey
yet again,
stiff from the saddle,
weary of desert storms,
bored of the incessant jangle
of camel harnesses
and of the predictable plod
of beasts of burden.
The dromedaries bend,
drop to their knees,
spitting and snorting
while travelers dismount
and disgruntled boys
unload coffers brought from afar.
The star rests
in its customary place,
illuminating the night,
beckoning with brilliance
as magi carry kingly gifts
to the peasant child
whom they have found
on Epiphanies past.
Once over the threshold,
they, too, bend,
drop to the ground,

offering themselves
in silent adoration
to the one whose name
they read in the skies.
And when, light of heart,
they return East,
they know that new signs
will summon them once more,
that new routes and caravans
will lead them
through dark days
without end.

And so the wisemen . . .

God's Presence

Upon you the Lord shines and over you appears God's glory. *Isaiah 60:2*

What is this wondrous light that pierces through darkness, tearing the shroud that covers earth and its people? What is this wondrous light that sets camel caravans in motions, with gift-bearers—men, women, children—singing praise? What is this wondrous light that beckons astrologers from afar and leads them through hostile deserts to the birthplace of a child? What is this wondrous light that shines in the depth of our hearts, filling the darkest recesses with radiance beyond all telling?

This light, this wondrous light, is our assurance that God is with us. This light is our guarantee that love is stronger than hatred, that beauty is more powerful than ugliness, that goodness will prevail over evil. This light, this wondrous light, offers more than a hint of God's presence. It overwhelms us, entices us, woos us and claims us for its own. Let us welcome this light; let us shine with its brilliance.

Shine upon us, Lord, that our hearts may sing praise.

A Risky Venture

I was a shepherd and a dresser of sycamores.
Amos 7:14

There is a wistful note in Amos' words as he recalls his former way of life. Sheep and trees had been the stuff of his days; sheep and trees gave him his identity and economic security. There was nothing pretentious about his work, nothing that would set him apart from his neighbors and relatives or give him cause to "think big" for the future. Life was ordinary, predictable and safe. Then, Scripture tells us, God roared like a mighty lion, shattering all certainties, startling Amos into prophetic ministry.

When life is going along at a comfortable pace, God seems to have a habit of intervening and asking us to do more. Sometimes we have to leave what is familiar and venture out into risk and ambiguity. At such times, we may need to let go of our definitions of self and allow ourselves to grow into whomever God wants us to be. Whether God whispers or roars, it is always an invitation to deep adventure.

O God, grant me the courage to act decisively when I hear your call.

Draw Near

He pitied them, for they were like sheep without a shepherd. *Mark 6:34*

How the crowd must have shoved and jostled! How they must have hurried along, frantic for a glimpse of the Teacher! In their poverty, in their emptiness, they hungered to be in his presence and to feed upon his words. They couldn't imagine that Jesus might have needs of his own—to be alone with his friends, for example, or to have time to eat and rest. They knew only their own needs, their own pain, and so they hounded him down until they found him.

Jesus responded with compassion. He looked at the lost and the lowly and saw in them what he sees in each of us—a blend of confusion, agitation, desperation, expectancy. He saw the same world-weariness, fatigue and brokenness that line our faces 2,000 years later. Gently, he invited them to draw near and to make themselves comfortable. Gently, he invites us to draw near also, that we, too, may find comfort in his shepherding.

Draw near to us, Lord, that we may find safety.

Love One Another

We have observed his star at its rising, and have come to pay him homage.

Matthew 2:2

The astrologers from the East witnessed a special star and risked all to discover its meaning. They left behind comfort and security and headed into the unknown, certain that whatever meaning they discovered would be worth the journey. And the closer they drew to their destination, the more the star illuminated the night, beckoning with its brilliance.

We are also on a journey which demands risk-taking. Though we may not have a star as a guide, we must answer this question: How is the Christ Child present in our midst? The astrologers found the answer in Bethlehem. We are to create Bethlehems wherever we are; we are to make Christ present wherever we find ourselves. May the Christ Child be present in the way we love one another, as well as deep within our hearts.

Loving God, show us the way to your heart.

Was It Not Enough?

Was it not enough
that God so desired us
that once upon a time
the Word
broke through silence
and entered history,
speaking promise,
shaping future
with syllables of love?

Was it not enough
that God came down
to be with us,
to take on human form
that we might cherish
in the Child
the One who sang creation
out of chaos,
calling stars and moon by name,
outshining the sun?

Was it not enough
that God entered
the poverty of life,
humble peasant
of rich lineage,

born in a stable
that we might find
majesty in straw?

Perhaps it was too much
for humankind—
perhaps divine extravagance
set hearts trembling
with the fear
of what might be expected
in return—
too much loving from hearts squeezed dry
by selfishness and greed?

Perhaps, when all is said and done,
magic and glitter
are more enticing than mystery.
Perhaps elves and dancing bears
are easier to grasp
than God's great love.
Perhaps food and drink
are more palatable
than a homeless babe
who asks for nothing less
than an empty heart
to house him. . . .

Was it not enough?

A Flame Of Faith

Stir into flame the gift of God. *2 Timothy 1:6*

Faith has less to do with what we believe than with what we are.

Faith, God's gift to us, is that fire within, one and the same as the fire of God. Through faith, we participate in God's life. Through faith, we align ourselves with God's power and so can accomplish the seemingly impossible—as Jesus suggests in his image of the uprooted mulberry tree (Lk. 17:6). Our faith, then, is our strength, our very life.

The flame of faith does not dance on its own, unattended. Ignited at baptism, it needs to be prodded and coaxed into greater intensity. Without constant care, it flickers and dies, burning itself out because the source of its energy has not been renewed. Our task, St. Paul reminds us, is to be caretakers of the sacred flame, guardians of the fire. We are to keep watch, day and night, fanning the flame so that it burns with increasing vigor; fanning the flame so that the kindling can catch, too.

Come, fire of God, burn in us that the world may blaze with your love.

Ever New

Rise up in splendor, Jerusalem! Your light has come. *Isaiah 60:1*

On the Feast of the Epiphany, the world has already begun its return to ordinary time. Churches may still be decked with Christmas radiance, but in many households, colored lights lie coiled in darkness and tinsel glitters around the edges of garbage cans. We listen to the Gospel narrative of the Magi and sing carols, but we know in our hearts that Christmas time has come and gone.

The Magi also return to ordinary time—to the tedious journey across barren deserts, to patterns of living they had left behind. For them, however, nothing can be exactly the same, for they have been changed by the light of their star. May we, too, carry the light of Christmas into the new year and beyond. May Christ be reborn daily in our hearts!

O Lord, our light, help us to see you even on the most ordinary of days.

ORDINARY TIME

And yet it is precisely in the simplest moments of our lives that we tend to find God . . .

When my second book of poems was ready for publication, I was disappointed to learn that the title I had selected—*Ordinary Time*—was already listed in Books in Print and could therefore not be used. Part of my own spiritual journey had involved learning to recognize God's presence in the ordinary events of life, instead of only in the "mountain top" experiences. Since my poetry celebrated this discovery, *Ordinary Time* seemed like the most appropriate title to go with—and yet I could not. Much to my relief, a friend suggested *Extraordinary Time* as an alternative.

I was even more pleased with this title than with the first. Whether speaking of the liturgical season or of daily events, we tend to dismiss the "ordinary" as humdrum, boring, colorless, empty, unworthy of notice. . . . And yet it is precisely in the simplest moments of our lives that we tend to find God; it is precisely when we have finished celebrating the high feasts that we can rest long enough to allow God to find us. In this way, then, ordinary time *is* extraordinary—that is, if we are perceptive enough to scan beneath the surface, to probe beneath the skin, to strip away layers of superfluities.

And so *Extraordinary Time* made its way into the world in 1988. It was a collection of my own thoughts, feelings, memories and theological reflections; it included personal pieces and poems which captured the plight of the urban poor; there were tragic events gleaned from the evening news and angry tirades against institutionalized sexism and racism. There was no "controlling theme" to justify why I grouped these poems together; all that they shared in common was that they evolved from the ordinary stuff of life.

It is easy to locate the holy in a magnificent cathedral or in a place of remarkable scenic beauty, but the truth of the matter is that God is to be found wherever we are—in cities and suburbs, in classrooms and factories, in offices and kitchens, in cars jammed on an expressway and in crowded commuter trains. It is also a temptation to look ahead to a special occasion—a birthday or an anniversary, for example—as a suitable time for encountering God. But while God may be present on days of festival, God is also present in the here and now:

> For now
> is the time
> of the garden,
> the hour of holiness,
> the time to redeem
> from forgetfulness,
> the time of waiting in readiness. . . .
> Now is the time for cutting loose
> and disentangling,

for unfettering
and extricating,
for opening wide
the iron cage. . . .
          "Nazareth Sequences,"
          Woman Dreamer, 1989

Ordinary Time is a time for simple heroism. It invites us to receive each moment as gift, without expectation that something better is lying ahead. It challenges us to hear God's call in this very moment, even if it might be more convenient to defer listening to some future time. It asks us to consider saying, "Here I am, Lord," even if we would prefer to wait until tomorrow. Ordinary Time reminds us that epiphany moments can break through our consciousness in all times and in all places. It instructs us to examine our allegiances and to see what place God occupies in the fabric of our lives. It calls us to fullness of life and greatness of heart, to holy simplicity and to a spirit of detachment. Ordinary Time is the time of the greening power of God, that time when even the humblest blade of grass gives glory by being itself.

Amen.

Ordinary Time

The tree that bore
winter's festivity,
lending radiance
to the shortest days,
now lies forgotten
on the snow-smudged grass.
Strands of tinsel
glisten in the sun
while supple branches
bow to bitter winds
as they had done
before we hacked trunk from
forest roots
to carry our prize
home. . . .

Freed from nests and maple leaves,
this tree
was dressed in treasures—
bread dough ornaments
crafted on dreary afternoons,
bold paper chains
pasted, link by link, inexpertly,
fragile baubles discovered
in an heirloom box,
stuffed animals wrenched

from beds and shelves,
trinkets from overseas. . . .

The angels' song is sung,
shepherds keep watch once more,
and even the magi
have turned their backs on Bethlehem
to begin the homeward trudge.
Strings of fairy lights
lie coiled in darkness
while ornaments grow dull
in crumpled tissue;
gifts have lost their novelty.

All is packed away,
save this still-green ghost
which will endure
until the last dry needles
fall.

Respond Generously

"Here I am," I said. "Send me!" *Isaiah 6:8*

There is a child-like simplicity to Isaiah's "Here I am," a spontaneity and openness which we rarely associate with adults. There is no hesitation, no weighing of costs, but simply a willingness to serve. For Isaiah, God's call is enough.

Responding to God with complete trust does not come easily. Unless we walk closely with God, we may not even be aware of being called to anything more than our usual routines. We drown out God's voice with our own agendas. And if we do hear a call, we can respond generously only if we have learned to give and trust over a period of time. How we respond, then, depends on how much attention we have paid to God's presence in our lives.

Isaiah was a man of vision who walked closely with God. His writings reveal an intimate relationship with the God of whom he speaks with tenderness and compassion. Little wonder that he heard so distinctly the call to prophecy or that he answered so eagerly.

Open our ears to your call, O God, that we may respond.

Tightrope Walking

They do not belong to this world any more than I belong to the world. *John 17:14*

We belong and yet we don't. We are torn between following the conventions of daily life and taking a stand against them. We participate in the world, yet protest against it. At times we feel like rootless aliens; at other times, we take comfort in being part of the crowd, in doing the "in" thing.

No easy experience, this belonging and not belonging. We learn to compromise so that we can survive—we pay taxes, some of which go towards armaments, but we also try to support peace. We complain about the commercialization of Christmas, but participate in all the gift-giving rituals. We may boycott products of certain companies, but we buy from similar firms because the products make our lives easier.

Day after day we walk the tightrope of ambiguity. Our only comfort is that Jesus knows our dilemma. Let us pray that we may love our world without being seduced by its deceit.

O God, help us live in joyful awareness of your redemption despite the many double-binds in our lives.

Ready To Trust

He instructed them to take nothing on the journey. *Mark 6:8*

Jesus told his disciples to carry with them in their ministry only sandals and a walking stick. No food, no money, no traveling bag. No granola bars or juice for quick energy on the road. No portable radios, inspirational books or pads of scratch paper. No sweaters for cold nights or shorts and T-shirts for hot days. No first aid kits, maps, travelers' checks, insurance cards or list of emergency numbers. In a word, they were simply to take themselves.

Few of us would embark on a journey without "being prepared." We know instinctively what items will give us greater comfort or security. On our spiritual journeys, however, "being prepared" means abandoning our props and supports, and entrusting ourselves to God. It means learning detachment from things, places and even people, so that we have the freedom we need to see and love God. Whether we soar with God or walk with God, any luggage, however small, may work to pull us down.

Free us, Lord, from all those things which tie us down.

Pleasing To God

This people pays me lip service, but their heart is far from me. *Mark 7:6*

Jesus warns us that outward conformity to human precepts is no guarantee of holiness; it is the hidden recesses of the heart which reveal what we are. There, in those places known to God alone, lie attitudes and desires which may very well contradict our outward behavior. We need to place less emphasis on outer observances and to pay more attention to forming hearts which are truly pleasing to God.

By conforming to what church, state and local customs require of us, we can easily feel self-satisfied. In the world's eyes—and in our own—we are good Christians, citizens and neighbors. We can measure our worth by our observance of rules, regulations and traditions, and by all the extras we do besides.

"Doing," of course, has its place or nothing would ever get done and anarchy would reign. But we need to remember that it is our hearts for which our God hungers and nothing less.

Loving God, keep us focused on you, not on outward standards.

Prophetic Gifts

Pursue love, but strive eagerly for the spiritual gifts, above all that you may prophesy.
1 Corinthians 14:1

Most of us carefully avoid claiming any prophetic role for ourselves. Still, we know that prophetic activity is part of our baptismal commitment. Since the Second Vatican Council we have learned to speak with greater confidence about the "priesthood of believers." But being a prophet still seems much too remote.

The gift of true prophecy is the gift of the Spirit. It empowers us to speak all we have seen, heard and tasted of the mystery of God, so that others may be moved to believe. When we prophesy, we bear witness to what is real; we allow ourselves to become living symbols of God's presence. We carry God's word into the workplace, into schools and churches, into prisons and hospitals, into places of play. We may feel uncomfortable calling ourselves prophets, but prophesy we must—each in his or her own way.

Let your words resound in our hearts, God, that we may speak your name.

Infinity

Do you think
that you
or I
or anyone else
can embrace the

OCEAN?

We can touch
        rock
           sand
               water
          but
        never
      never
     never
hold all at once.

Our arms
are just not long enough,
our hands, too small,
the ocean, too big,
and the buckets,
too few . . .

A Constant Love

My sheep hear my voice. *John 10:27*

Your voice, Lord, guides me. Ever since I was a little child, I have heard you call me by name, beckoning me closer to you, inviting to share in your work of transforming the world. I have heard and I have followed, Lord, discounting the other voices, determined not to miss even the most subtle of whispers.

Your company has brought me joy, Lord. I have felt your presence at every step; I have trusted your shepherding. And yet you have not saved me from pain. Though I have followed faithfully, yet I have still stumbled and known distress. I have not escaped the thorns, brambles and cruel traps. You never promised me immunity from pain, Lord, but only the constancy of your love. Your hand holds mine securely. I know the tenderness of your embrace, and I believe a time will come for rejoicing.

Shepherd me, O Lord, into the joy of your presence.

We Remember

Such as my love has been for you, so must your love be for each other. *John 13:34*

For archaic peoples, the most sacred activities have to do with remembering. Their rituals, traditions and oral histories focus on the saving actions of deities and ancestors who provided models of "right" behavior. Through remembering and imitating, archaic peoples can retrieve primordial time and make it present.

Remembering and imitating are activities to which we, too, are called. Jesus' last words to his friends urge them not to forget the ways in which he loved them; they are to love others with the same generosity. Unlike archaic peoples, however, we do not simply have a sacred story to shape our behavior and attitudes. We also have our own unique experiences of the risen Lord. We need to remember not only the compassion revealed in the Gospels, but also that compassion which we have tasted and touched in our own lives. The love we share with one another, then, is not a love based on communal memory alone, but also on personal memory.

Remind us of the ways in which you have been present to us, Lord, that we may remember your love.

Trust Enough To Ask

For whoever asks, receives; whoever seeks, finds; whoever knocks is admitted. *Luke 11:10*

In asking, there is always the fear of being told "no." When we ask someone for a favor, we often preface our request with a statement of discomfort like, "I hate to be a burden, but . . ." or "I know this is asking too much, but . . ." Sometimes our discomfort is so acute that we don't ask for anything. We would rather manage on our own than set ourselves up for rejection.

Unfortunately, we carry this hesitancy to prayer. "I never ask because God might say no" is one excuse; another is, "I don't like praying for things because it seems selfish." Jesus, however, encourages us to pray for our daily bread, and to pray with persistence. He assures us that God will give us the good things for which we ask. If prayers of petition freeze on our lips, perhaps we don't trust God as fully as we think we do. If asking is painful, perhaps it is because we don't want to admit that all things come from God and that we have no control over anything. By not asking, we are rejecting the God who would lavish everything on us.

Loving God, give us the fullness of life you desire for each of us.

Made Whole

Were not all ten made whole? Where are the other nine? *Luke 17:17*

If there were ever an age when people needed wholeness, it is ours. There are obvious symptoms of fragmentation—broken families, corrupt courts, empty churches, teeming prisons, inadequate housing, mediocre schools. Then there are the less visible marks of brokenness—those wounds carried by people caught up in fear, rage, envy, deceit, failure, addictions, compulsiveness.

These days, to find someone who is "whole" is a rarity; all of us seem to stand in need of healing.

We experience healing in different ways. Sometimes, it is a long drawn-out process involving psychological intervention or medical help; sometimes it happens through a support group or a special friendship; occasionally, it just "comes," seemingly from nowhere. Anyway, we cannot claim the credit. As the pieces in our lives begin to fit more comfortably, let us thank the God of wholeness for restoring our health.

Holy God, re-create us in your image that we may be whole.

Surrender To God

Let tomorrow take care of itself.
Matthew 6:34

It is a characteristically human trait to want to be in control—to be so efficient and organized that every possibility is planned for. Thinking ahead, budgeting our time and setting goals not only give us a sense of accomplishment, but also save us from tension headaches. It is only in times of disorientation when all our plans fall apart that we realize how powerless we really are. Then depression and frustration set in; then terror holds us in its grip.

Competency and planning are not in themselves obstacles to our inner growth, but they can make us forget who is God. We imagine that we can surrender selectively—that we can pick and choose areas of life which we control while inviting God into the others. But surrender means accepting whatever comes our way in the trust that God will be with us, even in the most painful of circumstances. Surrender means taking one day at a time and accepting it as a gift to be reverenced.

Hold me, Lord, in the safety of your embrace; that is enough for me.

Be Yourself

Jesus asked him, "What do you want me to do for you?" *Mark 10:51*

Lord, there are times when I feel I ask too much. One day I come to you with long lists of petitions, and the next I want you to extricate me from some impossible situation or to move mountains on my behalf. Often, I feel too needy: I am embarrassed by all the demands I place on you, that I don't simply sit in your presence and be still. Somehow, asking always seems the poorest kind of prayer . . .

And yet when blind Bartimaeus cried out to you in his need, you heard his voice above all the rest and asked him what he wanted; he spoke, and immediately received the gift of sight. This story gives me courage, Lord. It helps me to remember your compassion; it helps me to remember that you offer healing. Like Bartimaeus, I must learn to call out and name what it is I most desire. I deceive myself when I think you want to hear polite expressions of praise and gratitude, or when I treat you as some remote deity who will incline a gracious ear only if I use the right formulas. Rather, you want me to be myself, and even if I demand, argue and implore, you want to know what is in my heart.

Teach me to pray from the heart, Lord, so that you will recognize my voice.

Love's Foundation

Let the word of Christ, rich as it is, dwell in you. *Colossians 3:16*

Relationships are often difficult. While we yearn for the ideal, we tend to fall short of our own expectations. There is often discord instead of harmony, intolerance instead of patience, resentment instead of forgiveness, cruelty instead of kindness.

As we listen to the Scriptures tell of "right" relationships, we may feel uncomfortable, perhaps guilty. There are too many people whom we are incapable of loving though they want our love; too many who would love us generously if we would only allow them to draw near. We think about relationships with brothers, sisters, parents and children, and find them sadly wanting.

Paul tells us that Christ is foundational for loving relationships. We need to forgive as Jesus forgives us, to bear with each other as he bears with us, to love as he loves us. If we live for Christ and in Christ, then the reality of his presence will shape how we relate to others; we cannot succeed on our own.

Let your word teach us how to love, O Lord, for our own hearts are cold.

The Real Self

He who loses life for my sake will find life.
Luke 9:24

Finding life, losing life—the phrases jar, making us imagine that life can be carelessly discarded or inadvertently discovered by the wayside. We tend to interpret Jesus' words about self-renunciation in life-and-death terms. I find it more helpful to think of finding and losing on an everyday basis: what is the life we lay down for Jesus' sake and what is the life we discover?

Each time we respond to the needs of the moment—at whatever inconvenience to ourselves—we are deepening our capacity for compassion, for being present to others. Each time we forget about chores and deadlines and surrender our time to prayer, we are deepening our relationship with the Lord, acknowledging that all time is his. Each time we strip away the roles and masks we hide behind, exposing the real self, we deepen our knowledge of who we are.

By refusing to be limited by schedules, formalities, regulations and self-preservation, we follow the promptings of our hearts and find life.

Lord, teach us to live in the freedom of your love that we may discover who you have called us to be.

Creation

In that time
in that sacred time
before memory
before story
before God cradled the earth
the Word was with God
speaking yet spoken
moving yet still
splitting light
from darkness
coaxing life from void
dancing over the deep
rippling waters with laughter.

And God said
"Let there be"
and there was
and there is
and there will be
God's Word is deed.

In our time
in our sacred time
we remember God's Word
spoken tenderly—
born of flesh

born of spirit
bearing God
blazing light.
And creation trembles
at the mystery
at the power
at the glory
for grace and truth
are ours,
Alleluia!

Life's Lessons

Both in death and life we are the Lord's.
Romans 14:8

One of the most painful lessons we have to learn is that we are not in control. Not only do events seldom go our way, but sometimes we are even unable to keep commitments important to others. We experience personal disappointment and may also feel we have let down family, friends, neighbors and co-workers. It is as though when we try to plan our lives, the unexpected intervenes to show us just how powerless we really are.

Confronted with defeat, we have two choices: we can either continue to struggle, planning for the future with every eventuality in mind, or we can work towards acceptance. If we struggle, then we are setting ourselves up for repeated frustration. If we surrender to unexpected events, then we are acknowledging that our lives are not our own and that God may be trying to speak to us through our experiences. Struggle saps energy and destroys peace. Surrender brings with it the comfort of God's presence—and occasionally the very things for which we were seeking in the first place.

Lord, help us to place ourselves in the safety of your hands that we may experience your peace.

Transforming Power

I came that they might have life and have it to the full. *John 10:10*

I have learned to be suspicious of any form of piety which defers happiness to a future time. I have learned to cringe whenever I hear people speak about the reign of God as though it were limited to future tense. And I am struggling to be less judgmental when I encounter those who regard this world simply as a place of trial in readiness for the next.

The fullness of life Jesus promises us is a fullness we can experience in the here and now, right at this very moment. It is nothing less than the fullness of love—a love based on intimacy in which each experiences the self as uniquely beloved. The transforming power of this love not only fills us with joy and draws us closer to the Lord; it also enables us to break free from all that limits, binds and stifles.

Jesus calls us each by name; in that call, let us find the music of possibility, the dance of grace and the rich, rich wine of mystery.

Lord Jesus, increase our share in your life that we may be truly alive in the present moment.

Living Sacraments

You are a chosen race, a royal priesthood, a holy nation, a redeemed people. *1 Peter 2:9*

"Chosen," "royal," "holy," "redeemed"—these strong adjectives became the basis for many of the liturgical reforms of the Second Vatican Council. They affirm the dignity of laity and clergy alike; they assert that everyone within the church has a right to full active participation; they remind us of our baptismal commitment to live in the light and to proclaim what we believe; they help us to understand what it means to be "living stones," "an edifice of the Spirit."

Four simple words. They reflect both our inheritance and our mission. All of us—both ordained and non-ordained—are called to be "priests," that is, to be sacraments of God's presence in the world. In John 14, Jesus tells us, "I am the way and the truth and the life." It is through him that we learn to be the community of faith that we are called to be; it is through him, too, that we will find our way to the heavenly reward awaiting us. Through him and with him and in him.

You have chosen us to be holy, Lord; help us to respond to your call.

Source Of Delight

God said, "Ask something of me and I will give it to you." *1 Kings 3:5*

The first thing for which I ever asked God was a shiny red cardboard suitcase to carry my books to school. I did have a leather satchel, but at six years old, one is conscious of what other children like: red cardboard was in, dull leather was out. I remember praying through the night that my mother would see the necessity of the purchase. The next day, I was the proud owner of one rather cheap, garish-but-just-like-everyone-else's suitcase. I congratulated myself upon my ability to pray and determined to do so more often.

At six years old, I was convinced that God had been actively involved in my new acquisition. Some thirty years later, I no longer imagine I can bend God so easily to my will. I no longer see prayer as the way "to get things," but as the experience of God's presence, a gift in itself. I have come to understand that it is when I bend my will to God's that I receive what I ask for. My accompanying delight has its source more in this union of wills than in what I receive.

May I desire your presence above all else, my God.

The Need For Weeds

Sir, did you not sow good seed in your field? Where are the weeds coming from?
Matthew 13:27

One doesn't have to be a professional gardener to know about weeds. Anyone who has tended flowers or vegetables knows that weeds appear overnight, creeping across the soil, tangling new shoots, choking delicate blooms. There is no getting rid of them: they crop up faster than they can be pulled, resisting sturdy hoes and angry fingers.

There are weeds in our lives, too—all the obstacles, setbacks, mistakes and disappointments that wear us down with discouragement, all the griefs that wound us to the core. God allows these bitter weeds to co-exist with all that is beautiful and lifegiving. Perhaps, in the scheme of things, it is the weeds which deepen our appreciation for the flowers. Perhaps it is those creeping, tangling weeds which help us stand a little bit taller and reach a little higher. Perhaps it is those same persistent weeds which help us develop roots so strong we can tap into the very ground of our being—God, now and always.

Help us to understand our need for weeds, God, that we may more deeply appreciate the flowers.

Invitation To Courage

At once Jesus spoke to them, "Take courage, it is I; do not be afraid." *Matthew 14:27*

Turbulent waters, violent winds, a 3 a.m. apparition—no wonder the disciples were afraid. Terrified of both the waves and the "ghost," they clung to the boat and to each other, crying out in panic. The storm raged around them and within them. Then the ghost spoke reassuringly: "It is I."

There are times when our own lives begin to rock precariously. The circumstances in which we find ourselves can be so overwhelming that we find it very difficult to function as responsible adults of faith. Instead, we allow fear to dominate, lapse into self-pity and become passive victims. The story of Christ walking on water invites us to be people of courage. When we believe that the Lord walks with us, we can find both calm and strength. Under his feet, storms subside, waters become still. With our hands in his, we, too, are empowered to rise above what drags us down, to skip and dance over lashing waves with laughter in our hearts.

Cast out our fears, Lord, with the comfort of your presence.

The Heart Of Faith

"You are the Messiah," Simon Peter answered, "the Son of the Living God." *Matthew 16:16*

There is no question about Simon Peter's spontaneity. "Tell me to come to you across the water"; "Let us build three tents"; "This must not happen to you, Lord"; "I will never lose faith"; "I don't know the man." Time and time again, the words burst out so quickly that one wonders if he has thought at all before speaking. There is a recklessness about his words which is at once both delightful and disconcerting. He speaks and acts as though thinking is irrelevant. Peter's proclamation that Jesus is the Messiah, however, comes from a place more significant than the head; his statement of faith comes from the heart.

It is easy to acknowledge Jesus as Lord with our lips, but making this profession of faith from the heart is more of a challenge. Too often, we speak out of habit. The words have little meaning and fail to sink into our consciousness. Perhaps if we repeated Peter's words frequently and reverently, we would feel them take root in our hearts and fill our whole being. Like the "Jesus Prayer," they could become a way of praying ceaselessly.

Lord Jesus, you are the Messiah, the Son of the living God.

Free To Forgive

Forgive your neighbor's injustice; then when you pray, your own sins will be forgiven.

Sirach 28:2

When I pray the Lord's prayer, I often call to mind the faces of those who have hurt me the most, especially those with whom reconciliation is impossible. I pause briefly and study the images which surface; then, when I am conscious of having a place for each person in my heart, I move on. "And lead us not into temptation . . ."

It is difficult praying for those who have wronged us when, like Shakespeare's King Lear, we consider ourselves "more sinned against than sinning" or when we still suffer from the effects of the wrongs inflicted upon us. But the forgiving heart is a liberated heart. When we reach out and embrace another in spite of our pain, the more deeply we understand the lavishness of God's love. We let go the desire for any righting of wrongs or making amends and simply accept the offender unconditionally. In this forgiving embrace, we are most like God.

Let us remember your mercy, Lord, that we might be merciful to others.

Change Of Heart

Tax collectors and prostitutes are entering the kingdom of God before you. *Matthew 21:31*

It is Sunday. We are seated in a cathedral, flanked by all the dignitaries of the local church. We, like them, have kept the commandments, fasted, prayed and tithed. As we wait for the guest homilist to speak, we are conscious of being upright members of the community; we silently congratulate ourselves on being Christians of good standing. Then comes the bombshell: as the homilist sternly gazes at us, scathing words break into our consciousness: "Punks, whores, bag ladies and dope pushers will make it into the reign of God before you." Too shocked to move, we try to make sense of these words.

The chief priests and elders of Jesus' time must also have been caught off guard. The message Jesus preached was that outward conformity was not enough. Only a radical change of heart would open them to God's presence. They, like us, needed to pay more attention to the quality of their loving than to self-righteousness.

Humble us, Lord, that our hearts may be open to your love.

Quest

THIS seeking
is becoming an obsession;
this waiting,
a lifetime's occupation,
wearing skin to bone
as I turn every stone
for the elusive Grail,
search dusty recesses
of my decaying home
as if for a lost coin
of great worth.
Diligently,
I scan stock market predictions
concerning fields of buried treasure,
investments in fine pearls,
taking tips from savvy merchants
on how to multiply scant holdings.
OUT in the distant hills,
there are still only 99 sheep
in the fold
and the spendthrift son
has not returned.
I bruise knuckles
against relentless doors,
grow hoarse
from repetition

But no one stops
to bind my wounds,
cancel my debts
or give me oil
to light night's lamp.

ALL
is dark
briar-tangled
barren

and so I wait

hoping

for a glimpse

of what is yet to come.

Desire For Healing

"Rabboni," the blind man said, "I want to see." *Mark 10:51*

Over and over again, I hear people admit that they are uncomfortable praying for themselves. They have no difficulty praying for others, but they find it somehow inappropriate to ask God for anything on their own behalf. A standard explanation seems to be, "It seems self-centered" or "Who do I think I am that God would be concerned with my needs?"

Bartimaeus knows better. The blind beggar in today's Gospel raises his voice above the noise of the crowd and yells, "Jesus, Son of David, have pity on me!" And Jesus, in turn, asks "What do you want me to do for you?" This is a question he asks each of us.

Healing happens because we desire it. Healing happens because we ask for it. Healing happens because we name our needs and because we trust that God does indeed cherish each one of us.

"Be on your way," says Jesus. "Your faith has made you whole."

Jesus, Son of David, heal us of all those afflictions which harden our hearts.

Saving Embrace

Teacher, doesn't it matter to you that we are going to drown? *Mark 4:38*

Several times I've almost drowned, Lord. Do you remember when I tried to walk on water and sank? I was six at the time and was visiting my cousins in Switzerland. If it hadn't been for that lame man's cane, I would have stayed at the bottom of Lake Geneva. And there was the time the glass fell out of my mask when I was snorkeling . . . and the time the waves carried me out to sea on an air mattress . . . and then last summer, when I got caught in the undertow.

There have been so many encounters with water, Lord. One could say that I have become expert at drowning. I know the tug and pull of currents, the roll of powerful waves, the helplessness of being tossed this way and that, like driftwood. But I have also known your embrace in the midst of storm. You snatched me from raging waters, calming my fears, giving me courage. You have set me on dry land, steadying my feet, gently leading me away from danger. In the midst of howling gales, I have heard you whisper, "Do not be afraid." For this I thank you, Lord, for this I praise you.

In the midst of the storm, Lord, grasp me to yourself.

Ready To Say "Yes"

Speak, Lord, for your servant is listening.
1 Samuel 3:10

Here I am, God, struggling to hear your voice among the many voices which tug, beckon and entice. Here I am, straining to hear your whisper among the many whispers which break through my dreams and reveries, cajoling me with their subtlety. Here I am, searching the stillness for signs of your presence and of your will for me . . .

I am ready, God. Speak, I am listening. Let me know what it is you want for me. Let me hear your word, deep in my heart. Give me the clarity to see and feel and understand all that will help me respond. In the fullness of your love, teach me your wisdom so my will and your will may be one. Remind me that it is in following you that I will discover my true happiness. Melt my resistance, God. Let me respond to your call. Let my whole being resound with "Yes" to all that you want for me.

Speak to me always, God, that I may hear your dreams for me.

Giving Everything

One poor widow came and put in two small copper coins worth a few cents. *Mark 12:42*

Who was she, this poor widow whom Jesus held up as an example to his disciples? We know nothing about her—neither her name nor her age. She is as invisible to us as she was to the people of her time. Perhaps she was one of those unfortunates whose savings had been devoured by the elders of the community. Perhaps, having no male relatives to support her, she was forced to make a living by weaving or by selling eggs and cheese. We can assume that life was a matter of survival and that she lacked the luxury of "extra income."

What can she teach us, this marginalized woman who wears the face of countless women we have seen and not seen? "Generosity" and "dignity" come to mind. She was not afraid to give out of her poverty because she knew this was an acceptable gift; nor was she intimidated by others' ostentation. Let us learn simplicity of heart so that we, too, may offer precious gifts to our God.

Expand our hearts, God, that our love may be limitless.

Good Harvest

Every tree is known by its own fruit. For people do not pick figs from thornbushes, nor do they gather grapes from brambles. *Luke 6:44*

The fruit is not always sweet. In spite of our efforts, the harvest can set teeth on edge or sour the stomach. In spite of all our best intentions, the produce can be bruised or even worm-eaten. Drowsy wasps may grow drunk on a fermenting feast, but we taste only failure.

Can it be that the spoiled fruit reflects our own lack of harmony? Perhaps. Can it be that the bitter harvest comes to tame our egos? Possibly. Can it be that we are looking at the wrong fruit—status, for example, achievements or wealth? Very likely. The fruits of the spirit—love, joy peace, patience, kindness, goodness, trustfulness, gentleness and self-control (Galatians 5:22-23)—are the fruits with which we should concern ourselves. They are the signs of spiritual maturity. They are the abundance yielded by hearts rooted in God. The other harvest is important, yes, but if it is the sole criterion by which we judge the effectiveness of our lives, then we may be in for disappointment.

Recognize us by the fruits we bear, O Lord; give us an abundant harvest.

The Needs Of Others

If they will not listen to Moses and the prophets, neither will they be persuaded if someone should rise from the dead. *Luke 16:31*

Who is Lazarus today? A street person huddling behind a "hungry and homeless" sign, dark eyes pleading between the ragged edges of a wool cap pulled down and a blanket drawn high?

Who is Lazarus today? A family evicted from their home after jobs terminate and checks bounce, leaving nothing for mortgage payments or medical insurance? Who is Lazarus today? Teenagers robbed of hope by dead ends in the maze of drugs, violence and fear? Who is Lazarus today? The elderly, cast off and unwanted, frail and lonely, beating time until time runs out? Who is Lazarus today? You? Me? People we know? People we choose not to see?

The rich man failed to see beyond his own gratification. Our challenge is to be conscious of other's needs—and to help, even when we are necessarily concerned with our own requirements. For this, Jesus tell us, is obligation, not mere choice. This, Jesus tells us, will bring angels to our side when the time comes for us to cross the great abyss.

May we see your face, Lord, in every Lazarus whom we encounter, that you may recognize us.

Waiting In Stillness

You shall love the Lord your God with your whole heart. *Matthew 22:37*

I am listening, Lord. I have finally banished all distractions and unwanted images. I have finally stopped fidgeting and wriggling, both symptoms of struggle. I am no longer staring at book titles or smears on window panes. Nor am I wrapped up in the torrents of words which too often consume my time with you—those lists of people whom I want to remember, things for which I am grateful, petitions for the suffering world. I am still, within and without.

In this silence, in this stillness, I wait to hear your voice, Lord. I have told you so often about my desire to serve. I have offered you my gifts, time and time again, hoping you find them acceptable. I want to be commissioned for some glorious task, to pour myself out that others may come and find you. But it is always the same: the only words I hear are softer than the beat of my heart. "You are the gift," you say. "I want your love—nothing more."

Let me know what to let go of, Lord, that I may have more time for you.

LENT

The readings of the season lead us into a landscape of desert and drought in which we are sharply aware of our thirst.

One Ash Wednesday, when the children were in primary grades, we had our own private rite of ashes around the fireplace. What with Peter and Alexia being bussed to school, the long commute to work and the geographical distance from our parish, attending weekday services was an impossibility. With great solemnity, we shared the readings of the day, burnt yellowed palms and smudged each other's foreheads with the sign of the cross. We were ready to move into the penitential season . . .

Ashes provide a fitting entry into Lent. They remind us that we, like all other creatures, will return to the earth from which we came; they signify that there is more to life than the material world and that we would do well to focus on Gospel values; they mark us with the sign of our crucified Lord so that we can re-commit ourselves to the way of the cross, that is, to the path of life. In addition, they call us to pay attention to those areas of our lives in need of healing, so that we can indeed "rise with Christ" at Easter. How much of all this the children grasped is difficult for me to know, but they participated as fully as they could, reflecting on ways in which they could "keep" Lent.

"Keeping Lent" involves more than austere practices and "giving things up." As a child, I often gave up candy for Lent, but would hoard all the sweets which came my way until Easter Sunday, when I would devour everything as rapidly as I could. I do not need to comment on the merits of this "discipline," but I do believe that in many ways, Lent "keeps" us.

The Scriptural readings of the season lead us into a landscape of desert and drought in which we are sharply aware of our thirst. Like the ancient Hebrews, we may lament the seemingly more comfortable places we left behind as we have gone forward on our spiritual journey. We may encounter trials and temptations, emptiness and loneliness; gripped by uncertainty and discouragement, we may find ourselves demanding signs or praying for instant deliverance.

But the readings also assure us that there is water in the wasteland: Moses strikes the rock at Horeb and water gushes forth, silencing the complaints of the unruly people; Jesus encounters the Samaritan woman and leaves her with such a deep sense of the spiritual well within her that, putting down her water jar, she runs to tell her neighbors. There are also stories of healing, forgiveness and liberation which remind us that the purpose of Lent is to lead us to new life. "I will open your graves and have you rise from them," says the Lord God (Ezekiel 37:12).

Water is a symbol of this new life. As we prepare to renew our baptismal promises, as we walk with the elect who will be baptized at the Easter Vigil, we need to immerse ourselves in the water Jesus extends to us. First, we must want to be cleansed from all that separates us from God, from others, from our deepest selves. By examining our choices, our use of time, our use of resources, our relationships and our desires, we can confront unhealthy aspects of our lives. At the same time, we can affirm all that we are doing well, so that we can see our failures as part of the story and *not the whole truth* about ourselves. Humbly, we need to acknowledge all that we are before our God, confident in the love and mercy which are always extended to us.

Secondly, we need to turn to Jesus as the source of refreshment. The journey to inner conversion is hard—fraught with such difficulties and dangers that our own strength cannot carry us across the drought-fissured landscape. Through prayer, however, we can, like the Samaritan woman, be led to new depths within ourselves, new sources of courage, perseverance and empowerment. Through prayer, we can discover that holy companionship which will carry us to the radical change of heart to which Lent invites us.

Be with us, Lord!

Ashes

You thumbed grit
into my furrowed brow,
marking me
with the sign of mortality,
the dust of last year's palms.
The cross you traced
seared, smudged skin,
and I recalled
other ashes
etched
into my heart
by those who loved too little
or not at all.

Seek Solitude

The spirit sent Jesus out toward the desert.
Mark 1:12

The desert is not a place where many would choose to spend time. Heat, sand and loneliness repel rather than invite. Accustomed as we are to air-conditioned comfort and incessant noise, desert silence seems oppressive. We fear not only physical discomfort, but also being alone.

Physical discomfort may be unnecessary for our spiritual growth, but solitude is essential. Without it, we begin to forget who we are. The craziness of the world begins to get to us and we are weighed down by a nagging sense of dissatisfaction. Prayer becomes perfunctory; our days merge in meaningless routine.

Lent is a time to seek out solitude—time when we can be alone with God, undisturbed by the pressing demands of schedules and the distractions of a complex world. Only by carving out a time and place for prayer will we experience the gift of the desert.

Spirit of God, guide me deep into the desert that I may find you there.

Desert Places

In the desert places
of my days
through chill gray hours
of numb apathy
and colorless dreams,
of endless waiting
for meaning
which seldom comes
when wanted,
if at all—
in those desert places
I cry out for angels' wings
to bear me high
above the dreariness
and the pain,
to set me
on a sun-bent course
towards the radiance
of the absent One
whose presence
I crave . . .

Know God, Know Self

You shall not put the Lord your God to the test.
Matthew 4:7

The tempter in this Gospel passage challenges Jesus to prove his identity. "Show me your tricks," he seems to say. "Let's see if God is really with you; let's see if you are really the Son of God." Jesus stands firm. Because he is secure in himself, he can discern that the voice he hears is not of God. He arms himself with Scripture and puts the tempter to flight.

Knowledge of self is foundational for the spiritual life. When we forget who we are, we allow ourselves to fall into the power of those who may make us doubt our worth or the validity of our experiences; we may find ourselves burdened by other's opinions or expectations. We begin to listen to advice that may be harmful and suddenly discover that we no longer know how to make decisions on our own. Gradually, we find ourselves losing our freedom and moving with the crowd; gradually, we forget the times God has intervened in our lives. Petulantly, we begin to demand signs.

Help us to know ourselves, God, that we may know you.

Dependence On God

I have witnessed the affliction of my people in Egypt. *Exodus 3:7*

The enslavement of the Israelites in Egypt is so much a part of our heritage that "Egypt" has become symbolic of a place of oppression. To be in Egypt means we need deliverance; it means to recognize our own powerlessness to rescue ourselves; it means to acknowledge our total dependence on God.

Lent is a good time for examining the Egypts in our own experience: those Egypts which we build up by our direct actions or by our indifference; those Egypts which we have to endure because others have inflicted them upon us. As we face the reality of our lives, let us remember the God of compassion who not only frees us from the bondage of sin, but who also breaks those destructive chains which prevent us from leading full and happy lives.

God of power and might, lead us out of all the oppressive situations in which we find ourselves.

Longing For Home

In their thirst for water, the people grumbled against Moses, saying, "Why did you ever make us leave Egypt?" *Exodus 17:3*

There is nothing romantic about the biblical portrayal of the Israelites in Egypt. They were oppressed by Egyptian taskmasters and forced into building cities. One can imagine the crack of the whip against sun-scorched skin, backs straining under monumental stone, cries of anguish, the moans of the dying.

But memory is selective. Once in the Sinai desert, with little but rock and sand, the Israelites began to pine for the green pastures of the Nile Delta, for the fleshpots of Egypt. It was not just thirst that they had to contend with, but nostalgia for everything they had known—for cucumbers, melons, garlic, grain, figs. . . . They were weary of manna, weary of freedom.

Like the Israelites, we, too, tend to be oblivious to our present blessings. We, too, tend to succumb to dissatisfaction and discouragement unless we are able to live as pilgrims at heart, longing for our home in eternity.

God, be our companion in the desert places of our lives.

All Sin Is Blindness

I know this much: I was blind before; now I can see. *John 9:25*

Everyone knew the beggar. Day after day, he shuffled through the filth and the dust, sightless eyes staring ahead, hands outstretched for any chance offerings. "See how he has sinned!" they would say. "See how God has punished his parents!" Then the beggar's eyes opened and he became living testimony to God's work. Instead of rejoicing with him, however, the religious leaders tried to discredit the miracle; because they lacked interior vision, they refused to see the obvious.

It is too easy for us to denounce the Pharisees in the narrative, too easy for us to name them the "sinners" of the story. All sin is a matter of blindness. Whenever our own prejudices and fears blind us to what is "real" about ourselves, about others, about the situations in which we find ourselves, then we, too, are morally blind; then we, too, are in need of healing.

Lord, open our eyes that we may see as you see, that we may see the good and the bad.

Grasping Grace

The untouchables
knew how to ask
for divine favor:
blighted from birth
or afflicted
by the unexpected,
this ragged band
of mendicants
grasped at grace,
finding wholeness
in spittle-paste, dust,
the fringe of a cloak.
These suppliants
groaned agony
not words—
no polite "vouchsafe,
prithee, please, do,
be so good as,
for mercy's sake"
but primal screams
which rent the heart
and opened heavens doors.
Come, cadgers all!
We who would receive
must go a-begging,
naked and poor.

Refreshment Within

Give me this water, Sir, so that I won't grow thirsty and have to keep coming here to draw water. *John 4:15*

Weary of back-breaking labor, the dreary trudge, the blistered hands, the heavy burden and a tired heart, the Samaritan woman is ready for a change of routine. If this stranger—this Jew—can provide her with water closer to home, so much the better. After all, the dusty walk to Jacob's well is both hot and inconvenient and having to lower her bucket into the depths of the well is no easy task.

But she has missed the point, this Samaritan woman. The water Jesus offers does not save us from external tasks and responsibilities. Instead, it refreshes us from within so we can carry on without being overwhelmed. At those times when life seems too much for us, this water can bring us the courage to go on. At those times when we are bone-tired, this water can energize us and restore our enthusiasm. At those times when everything seems flat and God seems distant, this water can bubble within, reminding us that we are not alone, that God is with us, waiting to offer us new life—if that is what we desire.

Lord Jesus, give us the water of eternal life, now and every day.

Cracked Chalice

Glass of Mediterranean blue
bright with southern sun
and the iridescence
of a far away land
set like a gem
in a turquoise sea;
bright, too,
with red wine.

Raised to the light
it shines sapphire
still aglow
with the formative fire
which blinds, dazzles,
but gives shape.
Slowly, it turns
reflecting a thousand rays
of every hue;
eyes lower at its radiance.
For though the cup
has crazed
cracked
chipped at the rim,
it is still
filled with God's love
spilled for us

who know
what it is
to be flawed.

Examine Your Motives

Filled with the holy Spirit, Jesus returned from the Jordan and was led by the Spirit into the desert for forty days, to be tempted by the devil. *Luke 4:1-2*

As we progress on the spiritual journey, the temptations which lure us become more subtle—so much so that we may become oblivious to the "danger zone" into which we can so easily slip. On the surface, our lives may seem exemplary. We grow in confidence, no longer fascinated by sin with a capital "S." We find ourselves acting as spiritual mentors and empowering others, and we begin to delight in our effectiveness. Yet as we become more whole and holy, we can start to overestimate our own abilities.

Sometimes, we forget that God is the source of any power we have. Sometimes, we use our gifts as a way of proving ourselves or showing our superiority, and instead of serving others, we serve our egos.

Lent offers us the opportunity to examine our motives and to see whom we are really serving. It reminds us that neither possessions nor power nor miracle-working are guarantees of joy. It teaches that the Christian "way" is the way of humility.

Lord Jesus, let us always remember that you alone are the source of our power.

The Path Of Suffering

He was transfigured before their eyes.
Matthew 17:2

The disciples wanted to freeze the moment on Mount Tabor. There stood Jesus, dazzling as the sun, whiter than light, bright as a whirlwind of fire. There stood Moses and Elijah, sharing the glory. Babbling in wonder, Peter proposed three tents to contain the searing vision. Neither he nor James nor John wanted the moment to pass.

But what the disciples experienced was a foretaste of what was to come, not a state in which they could remain. They did not yet realize that the only path to transfiguration is suffering. They had yet to bear their share of gospel suffering.

Our lives are also punctuated by brief moments of glory in which we know God's unmistakable presence. These moments keep us faithful, give us courage and prod us on to great endurance. They are a promise of what is to come when the present is full of hardships.

Show us your glory, Lord, that we can look forward in hope.

Raw Power Of Love

This brother of yours was dead and has come back to life. He was lost and is found.
Luke 15:32

Hidden away in a side chapel of the University of Notre Dame's Sacred Heart Church, Mestrovic's "Return of the Prodigal" is a prayer cast in bronze. Utterly naked, the prodigal kneels before his father. He is weak, slight of frame, and stripped of pride by fall after repeated fall into wantonness and self-loathing. His arms reach up; his head tilts back, supported by the one to whom he clings, the strong one whose massive form enfolds him in sculpted security and compassion.

The father figure is compelling. There is no old man's frailty here, only the raw power of love—a power strong enough to wrench the sinner from the dust. One feels him drawing the returned son to himself. There is no reproach but simply a welcoming, life-giving embrace. What is depicted is the pilgrimage to healing that we all need to make, not once, but again and again. Only when we place our weakness before God will we find the strength and consolation for which we long so desperately.

Hold us, loving God, especially in our moments of failure.

Boldly, Come Back

Take the fattened calf and slaughter it. Then let us celebrate with a feast, because this son of mine was dead, and has come to life again; he was lost, and has been found. *Luke 15:23-24*

Let the feast begin, God. Here we are, your sons and daughters, daring to return home because we have remembered your love. Here we are, keeping Lent so that we can leave the pig swill of our lives behind us. Yes, we have strayed from your path and squandered our inheritance. Yes, we have forgotten who you created us to be and have degraded ourselves. We believe in your forgiveness, loving God, and we know that you desire nothing more than our homecoming.

Boldly, we have come back to you, certain that you will embrace us once more. There will be no reprimands or harsh words, no punishments or probing questions. Instead, there will be wine and song, laughter and delight. There will be garments of the best cloth, new rings and sandals—and of course, the fattened calf.

Thank you, God; let the feast begin!

Passage To Life

O my people! I will put my spirit in you that you may live. *Ezekiel 37:13-14*

Lazarus unbound is a powerful image of liberation: there he stands, still tasting dust, still smelling the aloes and myrrh with which he was embalmed, still straining to see through eyes which were recently sealed. He stands as an image of hope, as a sign that even in death's corridor, the voice of Jesus can summon us to retrieve lost time, to find life in the midst of decay. He stands as an image of the fullness God wants for each of us.

The Passion of Christ invites us to examine ways death may hold us in its grip. Perhaps we are shackled by fear. Perhaps we are bound by the desire to control or by the inability to see our own goodness. Perhaps we are shrouded in deceit, chained by despair, fettered by hatred. Jesus calls us to break out of our graves and to live; he calls us to that freedom of the Spirit which makes death—even death on a cross—a passage to new life. Let his call rouse us from stupor, unfreeze our blood, and quicken the beat of our hearts.

Give us your spirit, O God, that we may find life.

Dry Wood

I am whittled away
like dry wood
under a skilled carver's knife,
trimmed of superfluities,
pared to the core.
The shavings of my life
lie at my feet
and I stand strangely naked
beneath the singing blade
which strips, refines,
gives form,
leaving me quivering
like a thing newborn.

Trust In The Harvest

It shall put forth branches and bear fruit and become a majestic cedar. *Ezekiel 17:23*

The tender, fragile shoot becomes a magnificent cedar; the humble mustard seed springs up to shelter all the birds of the sky. The message is surely that humble beginnings do not necessarily mean humble endings. As Ezekiel reminds us, the lowly tree can be lifted high; the withered tree can bloom. So it is with the spiritual realm. So it is with us.

At times all our efforts seem pointless. We struggle, but seem to get nowhere. We speak, but no one listens. We build up, but others tear down. We are left thwarted and frustrated, exhausted and broken. Why bother? Why make the effort? The Scripture reading from Ezekiel holds the answer. Months, sometimes years, go by between the time of planting and the time of fullness of growth. As the farmer who scatters seed, we can only do what we have to do, when we have to do it, trusting that there will be a time of harvest.

May we bear much fruit, Lord, for your glory, not ours.

A Taste Of Heaven

I am the bread of life. *John 6:48*

We depend on bread. We need it for our daily functioning, for our health, for our growth, for sharing with others. So, too, we need Jesus—bread that is Word, bread that is life, bread that is the revelation of God. This bread is ours for the taking. It is waiting to be discovered in every moment of our lives and not simply at each Eucharist. This bread invites us to eat and find life.

Jesus becomes our bread when we allow him to enter our lives, freely and with no restraints. He nurtures us when we surrender completely to his love. He satisfies our hungers when we acknowledge how needful we are and when we invite him into our hearts. The Jesus we receive at each Eucharist, then, is the same Jesus who fills us with his spirit and who sets our hearts on fire with the taste of heaven.

Jesus, Bread of Life, give us the food of your presence.

Nailed

Good Fridays past,
I joined the throng
of solemn worshippers
to recall the death
that made a difference
to embrace the cross
of my crucified Lord.

Today, I would wrench
my hands
from the wood,
tearing flesh from nails
in my eagerness
to be done
with grief,
to be free
from the weight
of shadows.

Suffering Jesus,
see my hands shudder,
see them strain
for release,
jerking and pulling
this way and that.
tension knotting

pierced palms.
I would rip them loose,
cut the cords
that eat into my flesh,
leap down from this gibbet
and flee,
not turning back.

Outstretched,
bleeding freely,
open to both grace and pain,
your hands are still.
Marvelling,
I estimate
surrender's cost
and my clenched fists tremble.

Jesus Suffered For Us

They tried to give him wine drugged with myrrh, but he would not take it. *Mark 15:23*

Was the mixture of wine and myrrh a crude form of anesthesia meant to numb all sensation? Did the soldiers offer it out of compassion or were they following standard procedure, doling out mercy on orders? Perhaps they offered drugged wine as yet another insult, knowing well that the agony would be too intense for any drug to dull. It seems incongruous that the executioners offered healing resin to the one they were about to destroy.

Isaiah's Suffering Servant does not shield himself from the insults and injuries inflicted by his tormentors. He surrenders, letting them do what they will. In Mark's Gospel, Jesus also submits, fully accepting the sentence imposed upon him. He neither lessens his sentence by drugs nor proves his power by coming down from the cross. He yields to relentless cruelty, to the darkness of others' depravity. He drains the cup of his passion—and that cup alone.

Lord, I offer you all my heartaches and sufferings, mindful that you suffered all for me.

Love's Freedom

I have been crucified with Christ and the life I live now is not my own. *Galatians 2:19-20*

One of the paradoxes about the spiritual journey is that the more deeply we experience God's life within, the less concerned we are about outward conventions. Because the law of God is written in our hearts, we have no need to cling to tablets of stone. In fact, "right" actions spring from the center of the self. As Paul points out, it is faith in Jesus which enables us to transcend external codes and to live in the freedom of God's love.

The Gospels present many occasions on which Jesus ignored the conventions of his day. Physical contact with public sinners or the infirm, for example, made him ritually impure, while healing on the Sabbath violated the religious code. As we grow in the life of faith, we, too, will find ourselves walking in greater freedom. Being true to ourselves will become more important than answering to public opinion; allowing ourselves to be directed by the indwelling God will become our rule of life.

Liberating God, teach us to walk in your freedom.

EASTER

. . . spring will come, no matter how bitter the winter has been.

The power of the Easter Triduum—Holy Thursday, Good Friday and Easter itself—carries us into the Resurrection even when our own lives may still be rooted in Lent. As with all the liturgical seasons, we have no guarantee that our lives will neatly correspond to the Church's celebration: we do not automatically move from penitence to joy. Moreover, we experience death and resurrection on a daily basis, whether it is Advent, Christmas or Ordinary Time. The idea that Easter belongs only to the light of heart, to those who have thrown off their robes of mourning, to those who have experienced radical "conversion," distorts the mystery of the season.

The experience of the Triduum, however, can lead us symbolically into the mystery of Jesus' dying and rising, in spite of anything painful that we ourselves may be going through. Easter, then, reminds us that, eventually, light triumphs over darkness, boulders roll away from tomb entrances and spring will come, not matter how bitter the winter has been. Easter is our guarantee that we, like Jesus, will find the new life for which our hearts are aching.

Foot washing and Eucharist, plaintive hymns and the veneration of the Cross, Paschal fire and baptismal water all help us remember the presence of the Risen Lord in our midst. The sacred stories we hear allow us to leave chronological time behind us and to enter sacred history. Along with the ancient Hebrews we are "passed over" by the angel of death, leave the enslavement of Egypt behind us and walk through the parted waters of the Red Sea toward the Promised Land; with the Apostles we allow Jesus to wash our feet and then share in the feast of his self-giving; with those standing at the foot of the cross, we weep over the outrage of the crucifixion and cruel death of our murdered Lord . . .

The readings of the night-watch of Easter remind us that God our Creator *can* renew the face of the earth—by forming and reforming all peoples, by breathing life into dry bones, by replacing hearts of stone with hearts of flesh, by inviting us into the intimacy of wedded love, by calling us to the water of life. And then there is the wonder of the empty tomb, the women's amazement, the disciples' disbelief, the race between Peter and John to see for themselves, the resounding "Alleluia" . . .

Easter, then, invites us to find life in the midst of death. It reminds us of the inner journey to which each of us is called—a journey of trials, yes, but also filled with growth, if we allow the events of our lives to school us. It is not all Easter lilies, butterflies and straw hats; no, it is a time for heightened awareness of things as they are. Even our liturgical symbols of fire and water have destructive properties as well as life-giving ones: fire gives light, but it also purges;

water allows us to be spiritually reborn, but it first immerses us in the death of Jesus.

I think back to last Easter Vigil, when the Paschal fire leaped and danced on dry ground outside the church, scattering sparks among our feet as the wind fanned the flames. I remember—and it seems so long ago now!—our daughter's baptism by immersion and her screams when the water proved too hot. Our popular symbols also have their shadow sides: new clothes, eggs and rabbits, superficial symbols though they may seem, speak of our need to believe in immortality, to depend on fertility and to "put on a new self" because the old one is inadequate.

Easter is as much a matter of death as it is of life, and unless we recognize this, we cannot enter fully into the mystery it embodies. Through our religious rituals and family traditions, we express our belief that Jesus is risen, that spring will come, and that we, too, can be revitalized. This faith, this hope can be either the pious stuff of convention or the unrestrained joy of those who have felt the weight of the cross. We have before us life and death, and we must accept both.

Alleluia, alleluia, alleluia.

Wounds

In the glory
of your rising,
your wounds shine
like trophies
of great price,
dazzling the eye
with radiance.
As I gaze
into the hollows
of your hands, your feet,
and see the stripes
upon your back,
the lacerations
on your brow,
I wonder
at the injuries
you see on me
and whether
they will grace
or mar
my resurrected self.

Recognize me, Lord,
by the wounds I bear
upon my heart—
no bloody stigmata

but clean incisions
which pierce precisely
to the core,
beyond the reach
of healing . . .

The Presence Of God

I will not leave you orphaned; I will come back to you. *John 14:18*

A presence . . . soft, warm and constant...calling us away from activity into stillness, calling us away from schedules into quiet rest . . . a gentle, persistent presence centered in the core of self . . . quiet . . . calm . . . no struggle or petition . . . simple gratitude and conviction of God's love. This is how some describe dwelling in God's presence.

At the Last Supper, Jesus promised his friends that he would return in the Spirit. The condition for his return was obedient love; the effect would be the indwelling love of the Trinity. This part of John's Gospel is complex because it attempts to describe mystical union with God, a reality for which there is no adequate language. Our attempts to describe, to define this union are fragmentary; we can only experience what it means to live in God, not explain it. May we all experience it often!

Be with us, Lord. Fill the emptiness of our lives.

Ease Our Burdens

Stay with us. It is nearly evening—the day is practically over. *Luke 24:29*

The two disciples making their way to Emmaus with heavy hearts pondered all that had happened to Jesus. The stranger who had joined them eased their burden. They pressed him to stay, failing to recognize him as Jesus until the breaking of the bread . . .

Most of us know people who ease our burdens simply by virtue of being themselves. We press them to stay with us, rejoicing in their friendship. Somehow, their wholeness, their attentiveness, their ability to respond brings out the best in us. We find renewed energy, new directions. Their friendship helps us to grow.

But we, too, can enable others to be more open to the mystery of themselves. The gift we have received from others becomes ours to give. Jesus is risen, but only with the help of others can we keep the certainty of his resurrection in our hearts.

Stay with us Lord, especially when evening draws near.

Wounds

Look at my hands and feet; it is really I.
Luke 24:39

Jesus' wounds are the proof of his dying, the proof of his rising. As he stands before them, glorified yet bearing the marks of his agony, his friends can see and touch all that he has been through. No imposter, no ghost would take on the burden of those wounds. No one other than the risen Jesus could bring such joy and peace, and yet be so scarred.

Wounds can be a source of identification. They are not to be forgotten, camouflaged or ignored, but worn proudly like prestigious medals. They testify to who we are, reflecting all the physical suffering, the mental anguish, the emotional crises that have been uniquely ours. They proclaim that, like Jesus, we also have endured the time of great trial, that we have been washed in our own blood, as well as in the blood of the Lamb. They are our guarantee that a time will come when all wounds will be bound and when all weeping will be turned into laughter.

Welcome us in our woundedness, Lord, and heal our hearts.

Easter Prayer

Lord, in the glory of your rising you bring all things to newness. In this season of great joy, wash away all pain, all ugliness, all sadness. Roll away all the stones and boulders that block our paths, trapping us with their weight. Untie all the shrouds and winding cloths that limit, bind and strangle hope. Call us from our tombs that we may find the music of possibility, the dance of grace and the rich, rich wine of your presence.

Receive Life

"Take this," he said, "this is my body."
Mark 14:22

Take, I say. Receive a gift freely given. Accept my body, broken for the life of the world. Accept the cup of my blood, poured out on Calvary for you and for all men and women. I give you myself so you may eat and drink and have your spiritual fill. But you must take; I do not force myself upon you.

Take, that you may taste the sweetness of my presence, that you may feel the strength of my embrace. Take, that you may hear the melody of my love song, the words I whisper in your heart. Take, that you may carry me with you each day, from dawn through the long night. Eat hungrily of the bread I break that you may be one with me, one with each other, one with the world. Drink deeply of the cup I offer so that your tears might mingle with mine, so that you might drink in the reign of God. I will be your light in darkness, your food and drink in the desert, your life in death.

Take me, Lord, I am yours now and forever.

Beyond Signs

"So that we can put faith in you," they asked him, "what sign are you going to perform for us to see?" *John 6:30*

With its rock beat and snappy lyrics, the musical drama *Jesus Christ Superstar* highlighted the discrepancy between who Jesus really was and the Jesus the crowds wanted. What the people expected was a flashy miracle worker who could perform sensational stunts on demand. They wanted a magician rather than God.

Though we may criticize the crowds in the Gospel story, do we not also treat God as a magician at times? It is not wrong to desire and even ask for relief from suffering. Jesus did that in the Garden of Gethsemane. But we are amiss when we ask only for "signs," and we believe that our prayers "work" only if we receive what we ask for. Our faith thus becomes dependent upon *our* will being done, and we try to bargain with God as with a merchant.

We mature as Christians when we learn to look beyond "signs" and instant gratification, and start to recognize Jesus as the sign that God is with us.

What signs and wonders am I demanding of God in my daily life? I resolve this day to focus on Jesus alone.

Risen Life

Why do you search for the living one among the dead? He is not here; he has been raised up.
Luke 24:5-6

Often it is difficult to move beyond the Cross to the Resurrection. We hear the good news but remain rooted at the tomb. It is easier to comprehend Christ crucified than the cosmic implications of his rising.

Christianity is not a death cult, but a celebration of life *in* death and *through* death. Jesus' resurrection is what gives us hope that we, too, can be freed from all that binds, enslaves and destroys. It is a sign of liberation which promises that, with God's grace, we can move beyond the many "little deaths" we endure to allow the Spirit of the risen Lord to shape our thinking, acting and very way of being. Because of the Resurrection, we can laugh at the powers of darkness; as Paul reminds us, our lives are "hidden now with Christ in God," safe and secure.

Unbind us, Lord. Free us from the power of darkness that we may share in the life you offer.

Lazarus

My name echoes
down Death's Corridor,
resounds like a summons
across lost time,
penetrates my stopped ears
until I can resist no more
but must arise, reluctantly.
My sealed eyes
strain to see
but darkness clings tenaciously
like the stench of decay.
I taste dust,
smell aloes, myrrh,
want to scream out
that I am buried
and alive,
but my face is linen-wrapped,
my hands and feet tied.
LAZARUS! LAZARUS!
Stiff as a corpse
I strain to sit, then stand,
shaking off maggots
as I sway,
recognizing the voice
I did not think to hear again
this side of the grave.

LAZARUS!
Again, the cry,
rousing me from stupor,
unfreezing my life's blood,
quickening the beat of my heart.
The rock rolls and I stumble
towards warm wind,
rejuvenating spring . . .

Christ's Triumph

They killed him, finally, hanging him on a tree, only to have God raise him on the third day.
Acts 10:39-40

You lived with reckless power, Lord. There was no timid tiptoeing about but bold actions done in full public view. You never stopped to think of consequences or allowed yourself to be intimidated by those conspiring against you; rather, you moved with the Spirit, proclaiming the word of life, liberating those who suffered from the grip of darkness. You were the hero, battling the monster of evil single-handedly; you were the champion of the poor, the one who spoke words of hope into aching hearts. But at the end, Lord, it seemed as though you lost. You hung on that cross like a convicted felon, bloodied and shamed . . .

Then, on the third day, you shattered Death and burst from the tomb; on the third day, you destroyed fear and despair. The intensity of your living not only led you to your death but also to new life. You have triumphed over all that shackles and binds, limits and constrains. Your Spirit is with us, now and always. You are Lord of the living and the dead. Alleluia.

Shatter our tombs, Lord; raise us to new life.

A Message Of Love

I entrusted to them the message you entrusted to me. *John 17:8*

Sometimes, I take being a Christian for granted, Lord. I follow you out of habit and don't spend much time reflecting on the great privilege it is to share in your work. I get caught up in details and frustrations. I am bothered by my own imperfections and those of the Church. I feel mute in the face of the world's suffering. I miss the point that I am not simply a laborer or a hired hand but a friend.

It is a matter of friendship, isn't it, Lord? One doesn't entrust what is precious to strangers or hired hands. Your message—the message you have entrusted to me—is a message of love. My task is to make that love known to all those whom I can reach, in whatever way possible. When I remember that I continue your work, then my hands are more deft, my feet move more swiftly and my heart is filled with willingness. Help me to keep your word and, in so doing, to give you glory.

Let me serve you out of friendship, Lord, and not simply out of habit.

Live Jesus' Passion

Blessed are those who have not seen and have believed. *John 20:29*

Jesus' story was not the first story of death and resurrection to grip the human imagination. Accounts of dying and rising gods were popular in Sumeria, Egypt, Greece and Rome long before the birth of Christ. Because "remembering" was considered sacred activity, these tales were passed on from generation to generation, first through oral tradition, then by the written word. They became the subject of prayer and ritual reenactment.

We must do more than remember. For Christians, the challenge is to bring the pattern of Jesus' dying and rising into our lives. We do not just recall Jesus' passion, we live it, embracing the cross, uniting our pain with his, accepting suffering when necessary.

While we look to the resurrection as the sign of our own final rising, here and now we continue to die and rise, die and rise in ways sometimes so small and humble that we may not pay them much attention.

Jesus, my baptism united me with your dying and your rising. Help me to live that sacramental reality to the full each day.

With Us To Stay

They gave him a piece of cooked fish which he took and ate in their presence. *Luke 24:42-43*

A piece of cooked fish was all it took. In breaking bread and eating fish, Jesus proved himself to be more than a ghost. He was his old self, yet somehow new. He was what he had been and yet something more. He had died, but somehow seemed even more alive. His friends were filled with joy and wonder, for the impossible had happened.

For us it is not so easy. Jesus does not magically show up at dinner time and say, "Give me something to eat!" Nor does he dazzle us with his risen presence or display the glorious wounds of his passion. Rather, he moves among us quietly, invisibly, revealing himself in every human encounter whether we recognize him or not, speaking to us in the silence of our hearts, whether we hear him or not. Fish or no fish, he is with us to stay. Fish or no fish, he will not leave us orphaned.

Jesus, help me to recognize your presence in all the events of my life.

Brookend

Now the coolness, now the spring,
gone all craving and desire,
now the shade by waters sweet
without end

Now the anthem soaring high,
gone the fear of flight and dance,
now more joy, inspired strains
without end

Now the Bridegroom's healing touch,
gone the aching loneliness,
now the kiss, restoring life
without end

Now the Light, how searing bright!
gone the shadows of the night,
now the blaze, resplendent flames
without end

Now the glory of His face,
now the splendid feast divine,
now all love and tenderness
without end

Tough Love

The command that I give you is this: that you love one another. *John 15:17*

Roses on Valentine's Day and chocolates on Sweet-est Day do not mean love. Nor do birthdays remem-bered and anniversaries treasured. Clothes collected for Goodwill and checks to UNICEF do not mean love. Love has nothing to do with ignoring others' faults or suffering in silence because we don't want to hurt someone's feelings. It does not mean forget-ting our personal needs or supporting other people's addictive habits. In short, love means something more than greeting card sentimentality and movie romance; it goes beyond conventional outward signs of affection.

Love is tough. It involves seeking the best for others, even if this causes inconvenience or loss. It means accountability and challenge, sometimes even confrontation. It demands bonding as well as letting go. It thrives on mutuality, trust, fidelity, courage, kindness and patience. At some moments, love re-quires limits and boundaries; at others, total open-ness. And, as God knows, it is what makes us divine.

Lord, teach us to love in the ways you have loved us.

Open The Door

Despite the locked doors, Jesus came and stood before them. *John 20:26*

We are experts at locking doors. Our sense of self-preservation extends beyond locking car doors and house doors to locking the doors to our hearts. Just as effectively as we keep out thieves and vagabonds from our property, so we learn to keep out those who would extend friendship, if only we would let them. Sometimes, we even succeed in locking out God.

We are so familiar with the invitation in the Bible to "knock and the door will be opened to you" (Mt. 7:7-8) that it seems strange to think of God knocking on *our* doors instead. In the Gospel passage for today, Jesus, fresh from the tomb, doesn't even bother to knock but breaks through the closed doors of the upper room and through the disciples' fears. In his presence, they find belief and direction, the courage to move back into the world. From this point on, life must be all open doors, while locks and bolts become relics of the past. How happy we are that God's love is stronger than all the complicated barricades we are so good at building!

God, show me today the locked and bolted doors of my life.

Amazing Memories

And suddenly from heaven there came a sound like the rush of a violent wind, and it filled the entire house where they were sitting.

Acts 2:2

On Pentecost, the Spirit broke through the locked doors of the disciples' fears, empowering those present, sending them out into the world to transform that world in precisely the ways that they themselves had been transformed—through their friendship with Jesus, through their knowledge of the Father, through the gifts of the indwelling Spirit. Jewish pilgrims who had journeyed to Jerusalem to observe the festival were startled at hearing bold proclamations in their own languages. Peter's testimony alone won 3,000 converts.

If we seek the locked rooms of our memories, there, too, will we find amazing and astonishing events—forgotten places where the Spirit has moved and made a startling difference in our lives; times when the impossible has happened and when we have been empowered, transformed, sent out to do great and marvelous works. Let us revive those memories often!

Lord, may your Spirit blow through the closed doors of all our upper rooms.

Given To Share

All of us have been given to drink of the one Spirit. *1 Corinthians 12:13*

If there is any biblical passage that rings with equality, it is Paul's commentary on the gifts of the Spirit. Everyone, asserts Paul, who shares in Christ's Spirit belongs to the same body; everyone who has gifts to share received those gifts from the Spirit for the common good: in this Spirit, there are no distinctions of age, sex, race, handicap, ethnic background or socio-economic standing. All are one.

This radical text has become worn with familiarity. We listen but only half hear the challenge and the affirmation it presents. We nod our heads in agreement but fail to see the ways in which it applies to us. Do we recognize our equal standing before the Lord? Do we use our gifts to aggrandize our egos or to build up the body of Christ? Do we work towards the dignity of all or do we accept hierarchical divisions as the norm? Do we freely offer our gifts in God's service or do we hold back out of fear or false humility?

Come, Spirit of God, that we may hear your creative word and respond!

Transforming Prophets

The holy Spirit that the Father will send in my name—he will teach you everything and remind you of all that I told you. *John 14:26*

In the Hebrew Scriptures, there are several stories in which the response to God's call is "Who? Me? I am a poor speaker! I am too old! I am too young! I am a simple shepherd! I am afraid! . . . " Those who protested knew their own strength would be inadequate for the great task ahead. Only with God's strength would they succeed in their work. In the Christian Scriptures, particularly in the Acts of the Apostles, we see simple folk preaching eloquently, transforming the world around them. They, too, had to turn to God as the source of their ministry.

At times the tasks facing us far exceed our skills, training or energy levels. We find ourselves in situations in which we might well say, "Who? Me? Impossible!" And yet, in spite of our deficiencies, we are able to accomplish the tasks at hand. We may find the right words to comfort someone who is grieving. We may complete a difficult assignment on time. We may find the wisdom to resolve a painful conflict. When we allow God's spirit to work in us, then we can indeed rise above our limitations.

Spirit of God, be our strength and inspiration that your work may be done in us.

Stronger Than Fear

Lord, if it is really you, tell me to come across the water to you. *Matthew 14:28*

In storm and terror, the God of the Unexpected walks across water and calms both his friends and the tumultuous waves. Safe in the boat once more, Peter confronts his lack of faith. Yes, he had recognized the Lord, but the wind was strong and his feet had faltered.

Walking on water is a striking image for achieving the impossible. Matthew does not tell us how many steps Peter took before consciousness about what he was doing made him sink. Still, his faith, scant though it might have been, carried him forward through chaos. Faith is stronger than fear, stronger that physical limitations. When we put our trust in the Lord of Creation, we, too, will be empowered to accomplish more than we thought was humanly possible. We, too, may find ourselves dancing across the waves.

In times of chaos, Lord, give us the faith to go forward.

Emblems Of Victory

He showed them his hands and his side. At the sight of the Lord, the disciples rejoiced.
John 20:20

Lord, in the glory of your rising, your wounds shone like trophies of great price, dazzling eyes with radiance. Hidden behind locked doors, your friends gazed at the hollows of your hands, your feet, and knew you. They saw the stripes upon your back, the lacerations on your face, the gash in your side; to them, each wound was a mark of victory, a sign of suffering transformed.

Recognize me, Lord, by the wounds I bear upon my heart, no bloody stigmata, but clean incisions which pierce precisely to the core, beyond the reach of healing. Are they marks which will grace my resurrected self? I hope they are the wounds of one who has loved too much. I hope they are wounds which will help me enter the mystery of your own anguish. I hope they are wounds I can offer for the healing of the wounded world.

May the wounds we bear become the signs by which you recognize us, Lord.

Grace Holds The Key

... the love of God has been poured out into our hearts through the holy Spirit that has been given to us. *Romans 5:5*

We are made by Love and for Love. Sometimes, however, we fall short in terms of our ability to love. Fatigue, stress, disappointment and ill health are only a few of the factors which can wear us down, preventing us from reaching out to others. At times, I have been so over-extended that even the sound of the telephone has caused me to tense: "Who is it this time?" I ask myself. "A student in distress? A colleague needing help with a project? A friend who wants to chat?" For me, a hectic schedule can drastically decrease any generosity of spirit I might have.

But even if my initial response is limited, I am usually able to move beyond this—not through any strength of my own, but because God's grace opens my heart to the reality of the other person. Instead of focusing on my own needs, I find myself gradually drawn into an awareness of the one making demands on my time. Through grace, I find the compassion to love whomever God wants me to love in that given moment. This, I know, is nothing less than the power of the Spirit at work.

Holy Spirit, empower us that we may love with the fullness of your love.

Holy! Holy! Holy!

Holy! Holy! Holy!
Chaos has fled
like a dragon from the deep;
and the world turns,
turns in the hand of God,
caressed by divine breath,
cradled by divine love,
created within and without,
turning, always turning
on the axis of grace.

Holy! Holy! Holy!
Terror takes flight
like a shadow from the deep;
and the world burns,
burns in the heart of God,
aflame with mystery,
ablaze with energy,
consecrated within, without,
burning, always burning
on the altar of love.

Holy! Holy! Holy!
Darkness trembles,
flees from the invading Host,
and the world shines,

shines in holy Christ-light,
blessed by the Morning Star,
sanctified by fire,
resplendent within and without,
shining, always shining
in the fullness
of God.

Holy! Holy! Holy!
All the cosmos gives glory.

Holy! Holy! Holy!
Amen.

about the author . . .

Elizabeth-Anne Vanek holds a joint appointment
with the English Department and University
Ministry at DePaul University in Chicago. Since
1986, she has been a regular contributor to *Living
Faith*, a quarterly publication of daily Catholic
devotions. In addition to numerous articles, she is
author of three books of poetry *Frost and Fire* (Life
Enrichment Publishers, 1985), *Extraordinary Time*
(Life Enrichment Publishers, 1988) and *Woman
Dreamer* (Wyndham Hall Press, 1989). She has
also written *Image Guidance: A Tool For Spiritual
Direction* (Paulist Press, 1992) and has just completed a manuscript on image guidance and healing.

Also available from
Living Faith Publications:

I Am With You Always
Contains a rich variety of traditional and contemporary prayers in an easy-to-read format. Includes prayers and psalm versions by *LIVING FAITH* writer Elizabeth-Anne Vanek.
✓ Paper • 169 pages • $7.95 + shipping • **Code IA-W**

A Treasury of Living Faith
Features 365 of the best *LIVING FAITH* devotions from past issues. This quality hardcover book will provide inspirational reading for many years to come.
✓ Hrdcvr. • 384 pgs. $12.95 + shpg. • **Code TL-F**

Echoes Of Grace
This collection of devotions by Andrew M. Weyermann draws together the best of his powerful and inspiring messages for Christians in all seasons of life.
✓ Paper • 210 pgs. • $7.95 + shipping • **Code WD-B**

Shipping rates to a single address: $2.50 for 1 book, $4.00 for 2 books, $5.00 for 3 or more. To order, include title, order code and check or money order to:
Living Faith Publications
10300 Watson Rd.
St. Louis, MO 63127-1187